Source Books in
Landscape Architecture
6

Tom Leader Studio
Three Projects

Jason Kentner, Editor

Princeton Architectural Press, New York

SOURCE BOOKS IN ARCHITECTURE:

Morphosis/Diamond Ranch High School

The Light Construction Reader

Bernard Tschumi/Zénith de Rouen

UN Studio/Erasmus Bridge

Steven Holl/Simmons Hall

Mack Scogin Merrill Elam/Knowlton Hall

Zaha Hadid/BMW Central Building

Eisenman Architects/The University of Phoenix Stadium for the Arizona Cardinals

SOURCE BOOKS IN LANDSCAPE ARCHITECTURE:

Michael Van Valkenburgh/Allegheny Riverfront Park

Ken Smith Landscape Architect/Urban Projects

Peter Walker and Partners/Nasher Sculpture Center Garden

Grant Jones/Jones & Jones/ILARIS: The Puget Sound Plan

Paolo Bürgi Landscape Architect/Discovering the (Swiss) Horizon: Mountain, Lake, and Forest

Tom Leader Studio/Three Projects

Published by

Princeton Architectural Press

37 East Seventh Street

New York, New York 10003

For a free catalog of books, call 1.800.722.6657.

Visit our web site at www.papress.com.

© 2010 Princeton Architectural Press

All rights reserved

Printed and bound in China

13 12 11 10 4 3 2 1 First edition

All images © Tom Leader Studio unless otherwise noted.

Pages 96, 111 top, 115: photos © Florian Holzherr, Sky Space 2 by James Turrell

Page 105, 113 bottom, 114, 117 left, 118, 130, 131: © Marc Treib

Pages 106, 111 bottom: Images by Sean Ahlquist

Page 113 top: photo © Marc Treib, Sky Space 2 by James Turrell

Page 126: photo © Florian Holzherr, Sky Space 1 and Sky Space 2 by James Turrell

Pages 128, 129: photos © Florian Holzherr, Sky Space 1 by James Turrell

Editor: Nicola Bednarek

Designer: Jan Haux

Layout: Bree Anne Apperley

Special thanks to: Nettie Aljian, Sara Bader, Janet Behning, Becca Casbon, Carina Cha, Tom Cho, Penny (Yuen Pik) Chu, Carolyn Deuschle, Russell Fernandez, Pete Fitzpatrick, Wendy Fuller, Linda Lee, Laurie Manfra, John Myers, Katharine Myers, Steve Royal, Dan Simon, Andrew Stepanian, Jennifer Thompson, Paul Wagner, Joseph Weston, and Deb Wood of Princeton Architectural Press
—Kevin C. Lippert, publisher

Library of Congress Cataloging-in-Publication Data

Tom Leader Studio : three projects / Jason Kentner, editor.

   p. cm. — (Source books in landscape architecture ; 6)

  ISBN 978-1-56898-891-7 (alk. paper)

  1. Tom Leader Studio. 2. Landscape architecture—United States. 3. Leader, Tom—Interviews. 4. Landscape architects—United States—Interviews. I. Kentner, Jason.

  SB470.T66T66 2010

  712.092'2—dc22

                      2009053067

Contents

Acknowledgments

The quality and reputation of the Source Book series is due in large part to the continuous efforts and overwhelming talents of Jane Amidon. As editor for the first four books in the series, she shaped the example for others to follow and continues to be an active steward of both the Herb and Dee Dee Glimcher Seminar and Source Book series. Throughout the production of this edition Jane offered invaluable advice and council while generously allowing others a formative voice.

Without the generosity of its subjects this series would offer little beyond other design monographs. Tom Leader generously gave of his time and energy. From the first seminar session, he was open and candid with students, graciously discussing both his successes and failures.

Philippe Coignet's and Linda Jewell's contributions offer insight and critique that bookend the Conversations appropriately, adding much valued perspectives to the work from those who have known and worked most closely with Tom. Tom's studio colleagues were also extremely helpful with production logistics, especially Elizabeth Kee. A special thanks to Sara Peschel of Tom Leader Studio as well as Elizabeth Lagedrost, Marc Syp, and Jane Murphy for their tireless efforts with the installation of *Compost* in the KSA Banvard Gallery. Thanks also to all the students in the seminar: Cynthia Anderson, Saylie Bhate, Angela Bushong, Zhiguo Chen, James Hughes, Courtney Keys, Elizabeth Lagedrost, Jane Lanter, Goldie Ludovici, Tongsue Ly, Brian McVeigh, Erin O'Rourke, Elizabeth Ries, Tim Rosenthal, and Shan Wu.

The Source Books in Landscape Architecture would not be possible without the generous patronage of Dee Dee and Herb Glimcher and the support of many at the Knowlton School of Architecture. Special thanks also to Doug Sershen for his logistical support that helped bring Tom to campus. Finally, the editorial guidance and patience of Nicola Bednarek at Princeton Architectural Press is much appreciated.

Source Books in Landscape Architecture

Source Books in Landscape Architecture provide concise investigations into contemporary designed landscapes by looking behind the curtain and beyond the script to trace intentionality and results. One goal is to offer unvarnished stories of place-making. A second goal is to catch emerging and established designers as facets of their process mature from tentative trial into definitive technique.

Each Source Book presents one project or group of related works that are significant to the practice and study of landscape architecture today. It is our hope that readers gain a sense of the project from start to finish, including crucial early concepts that persist into built form as well as the ideas and methods that are shed along the way. Design process, site dynamics, materials research, and team roles are explored in dialogue format and documented in photographs, drawings, diagrams, and models. Each Source Book is introduced with a project data and chronology section and concludes with an essay by an invited critic.

This series was conceived by Robert Livesey at the Austin E. Knowlton School of Architecture and parallels the Source Books in Architecture. Each monograph is a synthesis of a single Glimcher Distinguished Visiting Professorship. Structured as a series of discussion-based seminars to promote critical inquiry into contemporary designed landscapes, the Glimcher professorships give students direct, sustained access to leading voices in practice. Students who participate in the seminars play an instrumental role in contributing to discussions, transcribing recorded material, and editing content for the Source Books. The seminars and Source Books are made possible by a fund established by DeeDee and Herb Glimcher.

Foreword

"What if?" I often heard these words from Tom during my three years as his associate in the early days of Tom Leader Studio. "What if" is an open-ended question that unlocks innumerous possibilities for transformations, forms, and scenarios. It goes beyond easy answers, well-known shapes, or any sort of design logic or method. This two-word sentence is more than a question; it is a philosophical statement in Tom Leader's practice.

Tom's training at UC Berkeley in the 1970s was much about design at the service of the environment and socially driven formulas borrowed from Christopher Alexander or under the influence of Ian McHarg. This "green revolution," as Tom likes to call it, established a clear hierarchy between nature and man—the green revolution promoted the social act versus the individual one. In this regard, the landscape architect had to follow nature's principles by adding the least possible elements to the existing green fabric.

Moving on to Harvard University and studying under Peter Walker and Martha Schwartz forced Tom to think in a different way. Walker and Schwartz taught two sets of influences that were linked together: artifice and geometry, and criticism and humor. For once, landscape was considered as a visual medium produced by unique, individual acts that are subject to the laws of composition and the need for intention—just like art. The underlying fundamental principle was the idea that one needed to objectify landscape. On its own, landscape was not perceivable except as a sort of endless continuum of matter that had no inherent cultural meaning. The only way one could assert the unique identity of a landscape in this situation was to clearly and sharply contrast it with its surroundings. This is where flatness, lines, grids, checkerboards, and stripes came in. These were tools that were so clearly unnatural that they unmistakably stated that somebody was doing something in the landscape that was not just functional.

As a partner at Peter Walker and Partners Tom undertook a series of projects (Longacres Park, Truly Farms, and Asahikawa Riverfront Park) that were quite large and situated outside of cities, with indefinite limits, moist grounds, few inhabitants, and limited budgets. Along with his personal site investigations, these projects were the beginning of a new redefinition of landscape design for Tom. "What if" became the starting point for a new set of questions, thinking, methodology, and working process where principles are not grounded in classical geometry but in larger forces, ranging from economy to ecology.

The first images that Tom hung on his office wall after establishing his own practice were not pictures of his successful past projects but a geological map of the Vesuvius, near Naples, Italy, retracing the volcano's successive eruptions since its origins as well as a diagram of the DNA sequence mapped in various bits and sequences. In both cases, the inner structure of an object is observed at physical and temporal scales. Each successive layer is a part of a global system, but is formally different from the one preceding and succeeding it and responds to a specific function.

These geometries reflect Tom's compulsive need to understand what is beneath the ground level and his desire to visualize the construction of a landscape since its origins—to retrace the evolution of each component and its interaction with others. In Tom's mind, there is an evident connection between this construction process and the shapes of a landscape. Morphological processes are continually in operation; canyons are excavated, deltas are created, abandoned or newly created land is colonized. The talent of the landscape architect lies not in mimicking existing forms but in identifying the operating systems at work, by measuring and mapping a landscape's past and possible evolution.

This approach reflects a need to ground a project in its historical geography but it also explains Tom's working methodology. His final concern is not with a project's history, the diversity of plants, or a specific shape, but his goal is to implement a strategy that transforms the landscape with visible and clear intentions.

Tracing and mapping, however, are only observation tools. The passage from a careful diagnosis to an active proposal goes through a transformation chain of modeling, slicing, overlapping, and assembling, either executed manually or digitally. At Tom Leader Studio these manipulations are not only figurative; they clarify various settings and the assemblage of elements by revealing the inner structure of a site. These tactile as well as theoretical operations become ultimately visible in the grading plan, which is more than just technical data. In it, the ground finally becomes visible. The design, however, does not sit upon the ground; it is part of the ground itself. It extends beyond the predefined site, borrowing structure from its strata and lending support to the performative surface.

Tom's quest is to situate his projects in a temporal rather than a historical mode. His goal is to measure spatial transformation within a broader continuity of change that goes even beyond human scale. The Fresh Kills (New York, 2001) competition entry is a good example of this approach using strata, because it contains at the same time visible horizontal elements (roads, forests, buildings) and a revealed overlapping of these same elements through time, which gave them shape and structure. These relationships reveal the dynamic changes that are either due to physical transformation by human activities or to the unexpected interaction between elements themselves. Tom considers this mapping of past temporal events a framework that makes design choices less hypothetical and coincidental but more conscious, with design being only a part of a broader system.

Once the general structure of the ground is established but not yet totally defined, a program can start. Ecology is one of the means that slowly transform the ground. Tom's design philosophy rejects ornament. For him, ecology is a metaphor for understanding the complex interactions between natural elements and culture.[1] In other words, it is a matter of scale—a landscape architect has to look at the intimate intricacy of ecology in order to maximize the transformative effects on larger sites. He has to ensure the productive collaboration between existing and proposed agencies in order to make sure the grafting is adapted to a site's specific uses.

All of these tectonic operations, morphological processes, and temporal site investigations ask the same question: how do we understand the world in which we live through the sites we experience? Tom's design questions the role of man in society and his relationship to it, understanding the users of his landscape not simply as spectators but as active participants in the landscape.

Philippe Coignet

Data and Chronology

Shelby Farms Park Competition Entry
Memphis, Tennessee

CLIENT:
Shelby Farms Park Conservancy

DATA:
Site area: 4,500 acres
Organic farm: 300 acres
Estimated Phase One budget:
    $75 million

MATERIAL PALETTE:
Restructured water system, tree
    cleaning and management,
    management of invasive plant
    materials, organic farming

August 2007
Tom Leader Studio is invited to take
part in the competition and submits
the first qualifications to the Shelby
Farms Park Conservancy. The firm
is notified of finalist status along
with Hargreaves Associates and Field
Operations.

November 2007
The first site visit is followed by a
meeting with the client group.
Tom Leader Studio organizes a
consultant team.

15 December 2007
First interim meeting with client.
Early concepts on physical form are
presented, illustrating the proposed
view lines and program (organic
farming, reorganized hydrology).

15 January 2007
Second interim meeting with
client. The presentation introduces
the topographic scheme, the farm
inventory, schedule, program, art
scenario, restaurant and farm center
design, and land bridge detail.

April 2008
Tom Leader Studio makes the final
presentation to governor, city mayor,
and county mayor in Memphis.

15 April 2008
Decision is made to award project to
Field Operations.

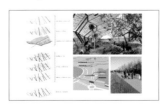

Railroad Park
Birmingham, Alabama

CLIENT:
Mayor's Office of the City of
    Birmingham
Private Partner: Railroad Park
    Foundation (Director Katherine
    Billmeier, Board President Giles
    Perkins)

DATA:
Site area: 19 acres
Phase One budget: $17.5 million,
    including structures

MATERIAL PALETTE:
Earth berms and excavation, lakes,
    streams, lawn, tree groves, recycled
    brick plazas, recycled curb and
    cobble stream pools, railroad tie
    boardwalks.

August 2004
Tom Leader Studio presents the
master plan to Mayor Bernard
Kincaid.

September 2004 to April 2005
Hiatus due to management debate.

November 2006
Tom Leader Studio signs contract for
Park Design and Documents with the
city of Birmingham.

December 2006
Kennedy & Violich joins the Tom
Leader Studio team as architectural
master planners.

Fall 2006–Spring 2007
Schematic design phase.

Summer 2007–January 2008
Design development.

April 2008
Discovery of land ownership
problems.

April–October 2008
Hiatus due to resolving rail land
problems.

November 2008
Tom Leader Studio presents design to
new mayor Larry Langford.

December 2008
The decision is made to redesign the
park with no rail land acquired: the
lake, amphitheater, and stream all
flip from north to south.

October–July 2009
Construction documents are
prepared.

November 2009
A new amphitheater scheme is
prepared by Kennedy & Violich/
HKW Associates.

August 2009
The Seventeenth Street restaurant
scheme by GA Architecture Studio is
abandoned due to budget overruns.
Tom Leader Studio designs new steel
canopy with "boxcars."

September 2009
Tom Leader Studio proposes and
designs an art vehicle called "Bivouac
Baby" for the park.

January 2009
Construction starts.

May 2010
Estimated completion of
construction.

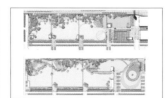

Pool Pavilion Forest
Napa Valley, California

CLIENT:
Norman and Norah Stone

ARTIST:
James Turrell

ARCHITECTS:
Jim Jennings, Bade Stageberg Cox

DATA:
Site area: 16 acres, 9 acres were
   modified

MATERIAL PALETTE:
Poured-in-place concrete,
   decomposed granite, lawn, deer
   grass, Dakota flagstone, grosso
   lavender, pre-cast concrete,
   trees (honey locust, sycamore,
   persimmon, Chinese pistache)

January 2002
First site visit, start of design phase.

March 2002
Tom Leader Studio presents schemes
to the clients.

June 2002
First meeting with James Turrell.

January 2003
Architect Jim Jennings joins
the team.

March 2003
Client reevaluates vineyards as a
space constraint, freeing up a larger
area of the site for the project.

May 2003
Construction documents are
prepared.

Summer 2004
Start of rough grading.

September 2004
Art Cave is commissioned.

October 2004
Bade Stageberg Cox is hired to design
the Art Cave.

February 2005
Cave construction starts.

July 2005
The pool skyspace is installed.

December 2006
Pool Pavilion is completed.

Fall 2007
Completion of construction.

30 October 2007
Opening party.

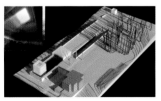

Conversations with Tom Leader

Compiled and edited by Jason Kentner

Jason Kentner: **You were a partner at Peter Walker and Partners for several years, and obviously Walker had a strong influence on you as well as on your contemporaries such as Martha Schwartz and Ken Smith. Who else influenced you in terms of landscape and design thinking?**

Tom Leader: Dan Kiley is one person that comes to mind. In the early 1980s, when I was attending the Graduate School of Design at Harvard University, Kiley held a guest lecture there. At the time we were still absorbed with the work Robert Venturi was doing in his practice and postmodernism in general. A few other students and I were invited to have lunch with Kiley after his lecture, and during our conversation I asked him what he thought about Venturi's map of the Mississippi, which showed the river as a plaza. He said, "I think it's ridiculous, completely ridiculous. You're out there on the Mississippi. It should be like the

St. Louis arch. It should be about the big sweep of the river and the magnificent scale of things." I wasn't completely surprised by his answer, but the force with which he delivered his criticism was really impressive.

Kiley went on talking about how, in order to be a good designer, you have to prepare to design. He said, "It's just like skiing. You can't go out and start skiing if you're not in good condition, if your body isn't ready to react. Once you've started thinking about which way you're going to go, it's too late; you're already on the ground. So you have to be prepared to design; you have to be conditioned just like an athlete. That's how I do it. When I am confronted with a problem, I just react physically. My body knows where to go and what to do."

Back then I didn't know what in the world he was talking about. But I think over time I've come to understand what he meant. It takes a long time for anyone to condition themselves to

Left: 2009 *Snagged* installation at the Rubin Center Gallery at University of Texas, El Paso, with Sarah Cowles and Alan Smart. This project included a regional investigation and installation looking at conditions of the US/Mexico border.
Right: Sarah Cowles, Alan Smart, and OSU students hoist the *Flying Ditch* into position.

be able to react in a way that's productive. Kiley certainly knew how to do that. More and more I find myself having similarly fast reactions to design problems, which I like. It's a little scary, too.

I was also influenced by reading about the artist Robert Irwin, particularly a book about him by Lawrence Weschler called *Seeing is Forgetting the Name of the Thing One Sees*, in which Weschler transcribed the conversations he had with Irwin. *Seeing is Forgetting* was published in the early 1980s, so it doesn't include Irwin's later projects, but deals with his early reductivist works and the way he thought and operated. One of the most interesting things I learned while reading the book was that Irwin was trying to achieve a state of boredom when he was working on his line paintings. He would go into his studio and stare at the painting for fifteen minutes. Then he'd fall asleep and when he woke up, he would look at it again and think about whether a specific line

should be down here or up there—by a matter of inches. Should it rotate slightly? He thought about these really simple, basic things, and this process would go on for days, weeks, and months, to the point where it became so boring that it was no longer about Irwin trying to realize some inspiration he had or a conflict that occurred to him. It wasn't about him anymore. It was about the line, the light, and the surface.

I drew a lot of inspiration from that for the very repetitive, compulsive aspects of the site investigations that I started just before going to Rome in 1999. If you just keep looking at something long enough, repetitively enough, it stops being cute or beautiful or anything at all. It's just the fifty-ninth time you've taken this picture and there's nothing but data. There's a lot of value in being able to achieve that state when working with landscape, because landscape is so latent and all kinds of things get in the way of objective thinking.

Tom Leader works with seminar students Brian McVeigh and Elizabeth Ries on McVeigh's material exploration of Karo Syrup and cheesecloth during the spring 2008 Glimcher Seminar at the Knowlton School of Architecture.

I've also never forgotten what Irwin says about horse racing in the same book. He wasn't making a lot of money from art, so to earn a living he placed bets on horses. He was very good at it—he never had a single year when he lost money. He was an extremely disciplined student of racing and would study all kinds of factors that most people wouldn't take into account. He would compute and keep ingesting fifteen to twenty different kinds of data, continually updating the information every five to ten minutes until the race started. At certain points he felt he could run his hand over the race, *run his hand over the situation*—in other words, there was a feeling that came from that process. It wasn't solely subjective or objective.

JK: **Intuitive.**

TL: Yes, it was intuitive. Because intuition is the computation of all those factors combined with

what he felt one way or another. That was Irwin's basis for action. He was almost always right, or right enough that he could make a living from it. I never forgot this idea of running your hand over a situation. It's similar to the type of conditioning that Kiley was talking about but more influential in terms of a rigorous or even compulsive design process.

JK: **When you look at a problem or site so instinctively, how do you test your intuition?**

TL: If your idea is not logical or functional enough, then you probably have the wrong intuition or reaction. But generally I tend to trust those initial instincts. Like Kiley said, you are reacting in a quick physical way to your sense of the issues at hand. If you can't make your idea work in terms of moving people from here to there and allowing things to grow and develop in a rational, workable, sustainable way, then maybe there was something wrong with that initial idea. The opposite, however—to bring a concept or a preconception of the principles to the place—never works for me at all. It's too constraining and repressive of the initial physical reaction in the Dan Kiley skiing way.

JK: **Your story about probing Kiley for a response to postmodernism makes me curious about your time with Peter Walker and how his office responded to the evolution of landscape through the 1990s and the beginning of this decade. What was your experience there and how did you process those experiences as you started your own practice?**

TL: Shortly after graduating from Berkeley in 1978 I did an internship at the SWA Group, which was at a time when Peter had just recently left the firm to teach at Harvard. The summer during my internship he came back from Cambridge with Martha Schwartz, who was still a student, and all the firm's interns went on a field trip to visit different housing projects in the Irvine area, Frank Gehry's office and his house in Santa Monica, as well as the Security Pacific Plaza in Los Angeles. It was really inspiring to hear Pete himself, whom I had never met before, talk about the projects, about where they came from, and what they were all about. He's really good at that. Suddenly there was a lot of discussion of the material world and how things fit together, which was quite new to me. Pete was concerned about composition, and people in the office used the word *beautiful*. I hadn't heard that before—it hadn't been part of the discussion when I was in school at Berkeley. Just before they left, Martha told me and the other interns that we should all apply to Harvard, that Pete would get us in. So I went to Harvard and two years later started to work for Pete at Peter Walker/Martha Schwartz, as the firm was known at the time.

I went through a lot of stages at Pete's office. I started out learning the craft, learning about grading and topography. Then I became more and more involved in the design process and after a while I took on projects on my own. The office spent the last half of the 1980s trying to bring the design work to a level of consistency, to codify the principles that had originated during Pete's teaching period. By the late 1980s it had become more and more clear what the response to a given problem tended to be. We knew what the tools were, and the tools related to lines and planes as an ordering device and the simplest way of expressing a structure or composition of elements. Where there was discretion to choose an organizational tool or a pattern to structure space, it was related to repeated serialized fabric of one sort or another.

JK: **Could you say that in terms of conceptual thinking there was not much attention paid to site?**

TL: I don't mean to give the idea that we were completely disconnected from the site, but the site was not typically what the design was really about. I got very good at working with topography, but usually the basis of the topography was to create a place where the design could be. If you didn't create an almost blank slate, the project's structure became muddy, and the design might lack the proper sense of scale or transition between spaces. I think we felt we were designing projects like Versailles. IBM Solana is an example where we did a great deal of topographic reorganization, but the final aim was to make a huge, totally flat parterre, with some very clear stepping and a few objects playing across this large plane, resembling certain aspects of the French chateaus. Creating projects like Versailles—achieving this big flat plane—

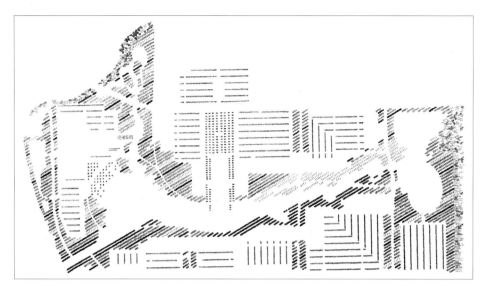

Top: The site diagrams for Longacres Park illustrate contrasting orders of vegetation and constructed wetlands.

Middle and bottom: Site model and aerial of completed project

Materials of site defy designed geometry and demonstrate themselves as a living landscape.

requires close attention to land and water and how it's moving.

JK: **How then did you begin to address site differently in your own work?**

TL: While I was still with Pete, I started working on Longacres Park in Renton, Washington, and that became an important project for me. All of the tools we had developed in the office worked quite well in the world of hardscape, concrete, and steel and stone, but Longacres Park was about mud and water, about plant communities and wildlife habitat, and about generating ecological function. I was thinking about an abstraction of natural systems, but we were still working with the same organizational principles and intentions. What defined this best was a detail model we made of the project, showing the lines of trees and wooden bridges and where they met the flowing streams and lakes and gravel walks.

The precise collision of these two orders was the essence of the project. I still felt the design was going to be considered successful or not based on its composition. I think that's how I was able to blind myself for a while to the actual realities of the site requirements. It wasn't until I went out there and saw the state of things myself—the cottonwood seedlings sprouting up everywhere, saplings and plants migrating wildly, growing way beyond where they were supposed to confine themselves—that I realized it was something alive and that we had designed the wrong things.

Around the same time Anu Mathur started to work at the office and she had a fascinating viewpoint. She was coming from Penn, where during the early 1990s Jim Corner was pursuing a different thesis in his teaching that was rooted in site. For Anu, the understanding and investigation of site *was* the project, and making objects or collages to represent this *was* the product. The idea was that this understanding of site should

Three Bay Area sites, including the Port of Oakland, Green Gulch Farm, and casting pools at Golden Gate Park, become subjects for Leader's site investigations.

become the generator of new thinking and new proposals. So Anu had a completely different frame of reference that related to everything about the site, about the nature, history, and culture that was not apparent on the surface. Between learning about this new way of interpretation and working on Longacres Park, which presented itself with a very clear, very different material agenda, I began to move in a new direction.

JK: **Was it this new direction that started you thinking about opening your own practice?**

TL: Pete was a major influence on my work, and I'm very much indebted to him. I learned so much about how to organize design ideas and how to express them in a material way. I don't know what my work would be like without that. I think that what I've done to date has been building on that foundation. I never felt that I needed to reject the work I did with him. In many ways I still rely upon aspects of that vocabulary, although I wanted to take it into a different environment, a different set of materials, and new ways of working. The idea for my own practice came later. The first thing I was looking for was finding my own voice. I knew that in order to have a successful practice of your own, you need to identify yourself, you need to know who you are and what your work is all about. That's possible without having any projects at all. It's really more about having a direction and a set of interests. I knew that the seeds were there but needed more cultivation on my own time.

JK: **How did you go about developing the voice you were searching for?**

TL: Initially, I did a series of site investigations and mapping projects as a counterpoint to the work I was doing in the office. These projects were my way of educating myself, or giving myself

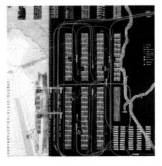

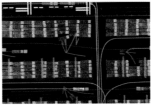

The study of the port reveals the underlying logic of the site related to the circulation and movement of container goods.

more practice at looking at and thinking about sites aside from what the specific design would be. As I mentioned earlier, the work in the office involved sites, but it was not about the site itself. At the time this seemed an interesting way of approaching landscape design: a way of postponing or completely deferring all of the physical modification proposals that you normally take to be the basis of your design. As I began to learn more about and appreciate that perspective, I realized that I really liked and felt a kinship with the minimalist vocabulary, but was frustrated by the codification of our responses in the office. I felt that it was removed from, or at least not fully integrated with, the places we were working on. What was the basis of them in that case?

So I decided to investigate different sites that seemed to offer a type of "vernacular minimalism": the Port of Oakland, Green Gulch Farm in Muir Beach, and the fly-casting pools in San Francisco's Golden Gate Park. In the office we might have shown a client or collaborator a site like the Port of Oakland or an orchard or a farm as a visual reference during a project as a way to rationalize an aesthetic minimalism—stacks of bricks or stones, or lines of vegetation. But, in fact, there's a lot more to it than just that. The regulating forces—the generator of the aesthetic in the case of the Port of Oakland, for example, are the movements of trucks, the systems for shipment, and the way goods are transported and loaded on and off ships. That's underneath what on the surface looks like a work by Donald Judd. Green Gulch Farm, a farm and meditation center run by Zen Buddhists, is another site where everything is clearly organized in lines and rows. It is very ordered, which relates superficially to aspects of our work in the office but asks a particular question. For me, that question was, "What about this row of lettuce?" What will happen to it? Two weeks later it will be something different, two weeks after that it will have been

The model study of Green Gulch Farm documents the changing conditions of the site and the precise ordering and schedule of the land's manipulation.

plowed and turned under. There is a whole set of sequences, movements, and relationships at the farm that takes place over time. Again I was looking for what was beneath the surface of the look of minimalism, trying to merge this new line of inquiry with the aesthetics and references of the formal thesis of Pete's work that I felt kinship with.

The simplest explanation for why I started the practice is that I wanted to find a way of merging these two perspectives together. I thought it would be powerful and provocative to make very specific physical interventions that engaged processes. The design wouldn't just be about revealing process as an end in itself, but rather about making a very specific intervention on behalf of a client's program or just a basic need. I think of hydroelectric dams as a comparison—water harvesting on the largest scale. It is a very forceful engagement of nature that helps us live. It has a vast effect, but it is dependent on rainfall and climate and soil. It is a clear interaction, an interruption of nature, but an interruption that doesn't last forever and can be altered or even defeated. It is an intervening force that influences the larger landscape. In a pretty brutal way, I think that's the essence of what we do.

JK: **What was it about those exercises that finally crystallized into a grounding thesis or example for the practice?**

TL: Farming became an important reference for me—the idea of cultivation, where a farmer has a clear program, where money has to be made and products have to be grown and shipped. The land has to be cultivated in a very specific way, and the farmer has to know everything about the climate, the soil, the markets, and must think about how to package produce, how to handle compost, waste, and so forth. Done properly, it is a very efficient engine of cultivation that requires a

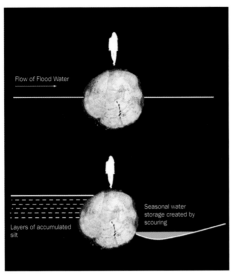

Flow of Flood Water

Layers of accumulated silt

Seasonal water storage created by scouring

Left: The concept diagram of Truly Farms shows how large log weirs would interact with flood waters and silt, creating an intentional cause and effect.
Middle and right: The interaction with the water system recalls constructed log runs used by loggers throughout the Northwest.

sensitive understanding of the site and clear intentions. That was what I liked about farming as a reference. If we're going to intervene in the landscape, it should be for a clear reason. That's still a fundamental basis for modern landscape. Farming is very simple but very sophisticated at the same time. So that principle seemed the clearest way forward to me.

JK: **Which of those early efforts to define your voice influences your work today, especially in terms of process?**

TL: Truly Farms is still a reference point for us. This was a project I worked on with students in Pete's office, and it was never built. Coming shortly after Longacres Park, this site was even more overwhelmed by flooding and influenced by the nature of the materials and natural systems. The goal of the project was to regenerate a flood plain forest on a large hay field that had been drained by ditches, but had previously been wet. Our ecologist—the same ecologist we worked with on Longacres Park—said to me, "Tom, you aren't going to be able to do what you did at Longacres. This is not an aquatic garden. You just have to let it be what it's going to be." But I resisted that way of thinking, because it lacked a clear intention. The site and project certainly demanded that we understand the nature of the materials and function of the site, but I still thought we could intervene somehow to produce the wetlands and the flood plain forest the project called for, while beginning to organize and structure it for human activity at the same time.

The strategy was to create a series of weirs, which were perpendicular to the flow of the floodwater, perpendicular to the stream. These large weirs would slow down the flow of the water and silt, and over time you could begin to build up a stepped topography to organize this flood plain forest, similar to a farming project. Just like the farmer had been growing hay, or whatever crop

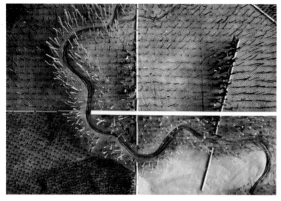 

Left: This model detail of Truly Farms shows the alteration of vegetation along the riparian corridor and how the corridor is influenced by the insertion of weirs and paths.
Right: *Breakout* recalls materials and sounds of rural life and pays tribute to the late Johnny Cash. Walls made of hay bales surround a maze of screen doors that evoke the porches and barnyards of rural landscapes. Fragments of Johnny Cash songs are played on speakers throughout the installation.

they had, we would be growing the wetland and the flood plain forest. People could then use the area on a human scale. I still think this kind of all-embracing consideration of how to organize and work with systems is a strong idea.

JK: **Since you started your practice, you have done a number of installation projects, such as *Break Out* at the Cornerstone Festival of Gardens in Sonoma County and more recently *Compost* at the Knowlton School of Architecture. How do these works influence your design thinking and process?**

TL: What I like about installations is that they are a way of continuing the idea of investigation and they allow you to try different things all the time. For us, that investigation is mainly concerned with the composition of the ground—what it is made of—which is somewhat similar to the interests behind our site investigations.

One installation that I've always looked back on, although I was disappointed with the physical part of it, is *Coastlines*. There were so many ideas embedded in it. I was asked by curators Aaron Betsky and Leah Levy to be one of five people to do an installation in the Revelatory Landscape exhibition in 2001 at the San Francisco Museum of Modern Art. The exhibition brief stipulated finding a site somewhere around the edge of the city and performing some operation or action that exposed the natural and cultural process.

The installation became a collaboration with Anu Mathur and Dilip da Cunha. Our proposal emerged from a very large geographic notion I had at the scale of plate tectonics: I was interested in looking at the alignment and corrugation of the topography as well as at all the urban systems of the East Bay that had altered the original coastlines. In our installation we wanted to track some of the parallel coastlines along the bay that were deflected strongly by this

This construction sequence of *Compost*, installed in the Knowlton School's Banvard Gallery, shows a strata of a lifetime's everyday debris.

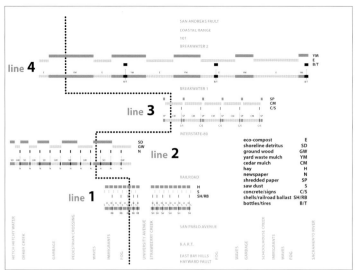

Map and diagram of faults in the Bay Area

large-scale trend. The final physical concept was really simple: we would make two layers of netting and fill them with sequences of materials and debris that were indicative of what the ground was made of at different locations where the original coastlines were altered. When the time came to do the installation, we had almost a mile of these double screens to fill. But while the installation was big—as big as we could make it—it still didn't seem as big as it should be; more importantly, though, it didn't illustrate the ideas sufficiently because it failed as an object. It didn't have the physical presence it really needed because we didn't finish making the object properly. We didn't fill in the nets to the top so you would really notice them. We thought that the infill would continue as a site process but instead people only heaved truck doors and other car parts onto it. I guess that's one site process. What I learned from *Coastlines* is that in an installation, the idea has to be strongly visible as an object,

even if it's representing or engaging process. Otherwise it runs the risk of being invisible and therefore useless.

JK: **How do you reconcile that observation with your mapping projects—projects that are not manifest physically in the way an installation or landscape is.**

TL: The point of map making, which I think is still perfectly valid, is to look at things that have no permanent physicality in themselves. What you're trying to represent, the information you're trying to compile and analyze, is completely changeable and dynamic. The only way to make something like that visible is to create an object like a map construction, or a collage, similar to all the mixed-media diagrams people were spending a lot of time on and thinking about in the 1990s.

A map exercise that did a great job of visualizing a series of dynamics is the map of

Top: *Coastlines* crosses borders created by infrastructure.

Bottom: *Coastlines* installed. The parallel lines of screen contain debris and matter of constructed ground.

Coastlines
Revelatory Landscapes   San Francisco Museum of Modern Art

Interstate 80 under construction

The *Temporal Map of Rome* shows the structural history of the city on layered glass plates, each representing two hundred years of time.

Rome that I created while on fellowship at the American Academy. It was a very simple process: I tracked different types of information—the location of rivers, marshes, roads, plazas, public buildings, churches—from the founding of the city to the present. What was necessary for this project was an almost blind compulsion to do it precisely and thoroughly without editorializing, so that by the end you had a very cold slice through all this data, through the life of the city. I found Roman scholarship in general to be much more anecdotal and heavily focused on very specific times, people, and objects, such as a single coin from 76 AD, so the project was kind of a reaction to that. Taking these objective, far-reaching broad slices of geography through time and then compressing them into one temporal map that showed how these places grew and expanded and contracted, was a more organic way of looking at the city throughout that entire period of time. Although the project was very simple as a process

and compulsive by necessity, the end result was amazingly complex and rich in terms of the relationships it revealed. The fact that the map was placed on glass and was completely transparent and the data was very consistent allowed for a reading that had not been seen before.

I still think the best use of mapping is to gain an understanding that can lead to any number of interesting perspectives. In our work we rigorously study all of the factors that go into the horse race, even though we don't always make a map. Like Irwin we become students of these elements until we can run our hands over the situation and make a judgment based on that. Usually, our work is not so much about what you design, but about what the basis of your intervention is. The value of installations, mapping, and site investigations is to have thought systematically, deeply, and compulsively, if necessary, about all the relevant data, which

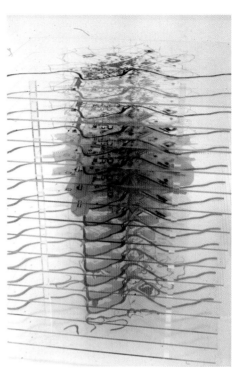

Model detail

isn't always just limited to site information. It's about what people are telling you, about specific politics. This process becomes less and less abstract as you work on large-scale projects, but it's still the same activity of taking so much in and studying hard enough that you can finally act intuitively.

Shelby Farms Park Competition Entry

Memphis, Tennessee

In 2007 the Shelby Farms Park Conservancy sponsored an invited design competition for its 4,500-acre property along the Wolf River outside of Memphis, Tennessee. The competition challenged design teams to envision a plan to unify the park, which was eight times larger than New York City's Central Park and bisected by the city's highway corridor. The proposal by Tom Leader Studio aimed to transform the park ecologically and culturally through the activities and actions of the park's users with the hope of providing alternative means of engaging community members from Memphis and surrounding suburbs.

JK: **A number of young practices such as yours have been able to shape contemporary landscape design discourse through a number of widely published design competitions. Do you think competitions continue to expand the dialog within the field?**

TL: Generally speaking, competitions are a good way to get known quickly. They are usually published, and if you do well and your ideas are provocative or new in some way, it's a very efficient way to get your name out there. In addition, you can test things without taking a lot of risks. That's always been the benefit of doing competitions. The chance of actually winning, however, is less certain, at least in our case!

Competitions have changed over the past fifteen years, though. The days of the big important open competitions like Parc de la Villette are pretty much over. Larger and larger entities are running them for more serious kinds of projects, and as the risk increases for clients, they look for something that is in between a competition and a traditional selection process where people are interviewed. These days during a competition you will have to compete to become a finalist and after that you will have one, two, or three meetings with the client, and these

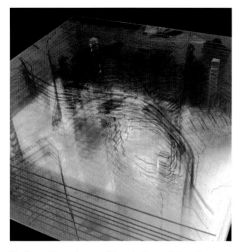

The Fresh Kills park competition studied an "alternative master plan" for the over two-thousand-acre landfill on Staten Island in New York.

presentations are part of the process. The clients want to see how you make decisions and what kind of things you decide to respond to or not. So the competition is not just about the product but about observing somebody through a process. That may be good for clients, but the more competitions are that way, the less easy it is for people just getting started to enter the picture.

JK: **What have your experiences with competitions taught you about yourself as a designer?**

TL: I think what I learned, especially in the early competitions, was that it is more satisfying to finally design something. While working on the Fresh Kills competition, with Anu Mathur and Dilip da Cunha, the three of us made a very conscious decision not to produce a master plan for this enormous project. Instead we decided to present an exploration or an investigation of the site. We wanted to create a resource that provided a key for understanding this piece of land, and from which any number of projects could then be spawned. I enjoyed working on it, but I had the definite feeling that it was more in my nature to design something physical. The site investigation was the right solution for this particular competition, but it helped me realize that what I really wanted to do is look for situations where we can make physical proposals for landscapes. There was definitely a shift in my practice at that point towards focusing on getting something built, something substantial that would test our ideas out in a physical world in a tangible way.

JK: **As you were shaping your practice, why did you choose to do so many collaborative competitions?**

TL: I was very conscious of the fact that we were tackling sites that were pretty sizable. Fresh Kills,

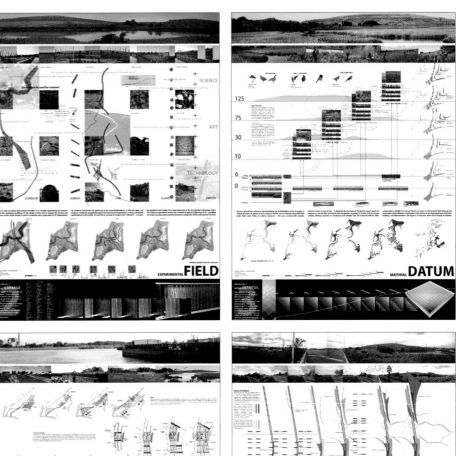

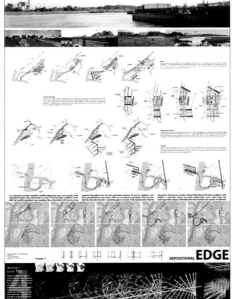

Mathur/Da Cunha and Tom Leader Studio's competition entry boards focus on transformative elements and places or means of intervention rather than presenting a directed and comprehensive master plan.

for example, was a huge project, and so was Shelby Farms, so I felt we needed other kinds of talents involved to be able to fully understand what we were dealing with. I did not want to take over and dictate, as much as help organize and coordinate several disciplines at once. Typically, a project involves geography, art, ecology, and architecture. So for all these large competitions we've either organized or joined some kind of group. Shelby Farms is the most recent competition we've done, and again we worked with a large design and consulting team.

JK: **Shelby Farms encompasses an area of 4,500 acres. How do you even begin to address a project of that scale? What do you "design"?**

TL: We had never worked on anything that large before but I didn't see why we couldn't. At first I was afraid that it went beyond design and was more a question of policy or just developing scenarios and bubble diagrams, which is not what I'm good at compared to creating designs that are spatial and based on the physical qualities of a site. Eventually, though, we found a way to approach the project. It became clear to us that if we were going to work on something that big, then the design had to make the difference: It had to be absolutely integral with a program that would begin to transform the park.

JK: **What was the issue presented by the Shelby Farms competition brief?**

TL: It was a large regional park competition but there was no detailed program. Each of the teams was charged with envisioning what the park would be. One big issue was that the property, which had been a large working prison farm since just before 1930, was divided by a highway that had been built in the 1960s. The competition was in part

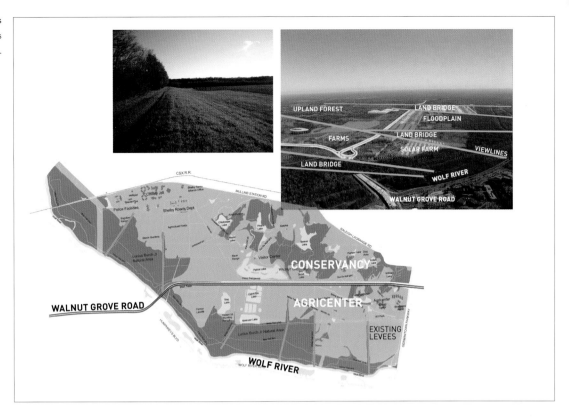

based on how to reconnect the two halves of the park.

During the late 1960s and early 1970s, Memphis's suburbs—like many other suburban areas throughout the United States—were rapidly expanding, and the city did a study for an arterial highway project that would bisect the property. At the same time the county government adopted the Shelby Farms Public Use Program (SFPUP), which was authored by a group led by Garrett Eckbo and sponsored by local business and civic leaders. The group advocated for routing the road around the farm, but sadly that was ignored.

JK: Did anything come of Eckbo's proposal?

TL: Eckbo's plan was only partially used. In the uplands he designed some facilities for a park the city built within the Shelby property, called the Plough Park after Abe Plough, one of the local civic leaders that supported SFPUP. This recreational

park used some of the smaller reservoirs and lakes that had been created previously to supply irrigation water for the farm's pasture and crops down below. In the lowland Eckbo designed a headquarters for an institution called the Agricenter. This center for experiments, research, and other supporting activities was supposed to attract large-scale agriculture to Tennessee, the same way you see throughout many Midwestern states.

But the big issue was that, due to commuter pressures, the city ran the highway, Walnut Grove Road, straight through the area, so it cut the whole site in half. As a result the Agricenter had its own domain on the south side of the road, while the north side became more of a normal nature-based park, which gradually came under the control of the Shelby Park Conservancy, an entity that was formed in the last ten years.

As a first step the team studied the site and established connections and relationships between conservation and productive landscapes within the site.

JK: **How have the two sides of the park developed since that time?**

TL: The upland park functions much like any metropolitan park, with families enjoying it for recreation. It also embodies more of the local environmental movement. The Agricenter on the south side was much more business-minded. In recent years it has been leasing out land for almost any vaguely related purpose in order to generate income. There were corn mazes, cow shows, and car shows. The Expo Center that Eckbo helped orchestrate is not only used for agricultural purposes but also as a venue for other kinds of shows, such as craft shows. The bulk of the property, though, is leased out to companies such as Monsanto and General Chemical, who use their plots to experiment with herbicides, pesticides, different types of chemical fertilizers, and bioengineered crops— all the kinds of things that the more progressive movements in agriculture are trying to move away from.

JK: **Was the competition an effort to bring the two institutions together? Who was leading that effort?**

TL: The Shelby Park Conservancy led the charge to design the whole site because it is all one piece of property, part of which the Agricenter is leasing. The conservancy proposed that the whole area be retained as one large regional park for the city and the county, and the Agricenter more or less agreed.

The charge that was put forward by the conservancy was to create one identity for the place, to come up with one park that is understandable to everybody. It was our job to figure out how to do that. I took that really seriously as a key issue of the project.

JK: **Was the park divided in any other ways?**

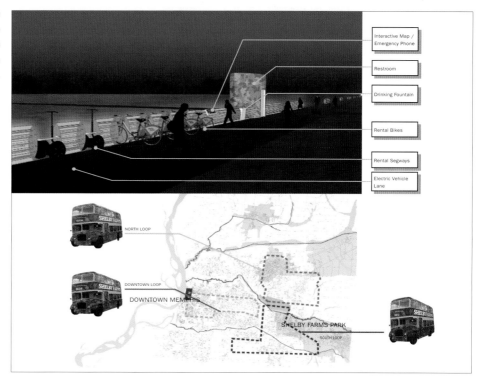

Interactive Map / Emergency Phone

Restroom

Drinking Fountain

Rental Bikes

Rental Segways

Electric Vehicle Lane

NORTH LOOP

DOWNTOWN LOOP

DOWNTOWN MEMPHIS

SHELBY FARMS PARK

SOUTH LOOP

TL: The site itself is divided topographically: there is an upland area and an alluvial plain, which slopes down to the Wolf River. The property had been subject to a lot of flooding in the past, but in the 1930s the Army Corps of Engineers lowered the river channel drastically and used the spoils to create levees parallel to the river to prevent flooding. They also created a series of perpendicular levees to resist the flows of any flooding that did occur. As a result the alluvial plain dried out and was used to grow crops when the site was still a prison farm. The construction of the road also interrupted the natural drainage patterns of the site.

The park itself is also somewhat removed from Memphis's downtown. The site is located in a suburban area, which is a twenty- to thirty-minute drive from the city. That distance has limited how many of the city's residents use the park, especially since Memphis is still a place, typical of many cities, where the line

between city and suburb is tied to social class and race.

JK: Designers have placed ecology at the forefront of so many of the other notable large park competitions such as Fresh Kills, the High Line in New York, and Downsview Park in Toronto. It's interesting to hear that there was also a social agenda for this park.

TL: I always thought that this should be a park for the entire city and the city representatives we talked to also emphasized that goal. It had to be for everybody, and there had to be some definite attempt at mixing user groups.

JK: How did you begin to address the physical and social challenges of the project?

TL: It seemed to us that the project required a clear but motivated, energetic program and

ENTRY POINT

CSX ROW

CSX ROW BIKE TRAIL

SENIOR FARM

SENIOR VILLAGE

AREA 10

CSX ROW BIKE TRAIL

AMPHIT

PUBLIC STABLES

CHICKASAW LAKE

ESPLAN

ART STUDIC

PINE LAKE

FLOODPLAIN FOREST

FLOODPLAIN FOREST

LUCIUS BURCH JR NATURAL AREA

WOLF RIVER

RESTORED MEADOW/ HORSES

RESTORED MEADOW/ BUFFALO

RESTORED MEADOW/ FESTIVAL GROUND

SHELBY RESERVOIR

EVENT LAWN

SAVANNA

FARM CENTER

ORGANIC

FARM GATE

HALL OF FLOWERS

FARM

ATHLETIC FILEDS

AGRICENT RESEARC

WETLANDS/ BIOMASS PRODUCTION

SOLAR FARM

CATCH'EM LAKE

WETLANDS/ BIOMASS PRODUCTION

FLOODPLAIN FOREST

LUCIUS BURCH JR NATURAL AREA

NESHOBA INTERPRETIVE CENTER

BIOMA

0   500'   1000'   1500'

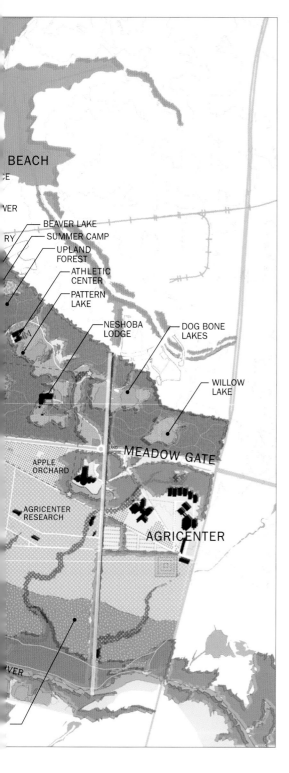

BEACH
CE
VER

BEAVER LAKE
SUMMER CAMP
UPLAND
FOREST
ATHLETIC
CENTER
PATTERN
LAKE
NESHOBA
LODGE
DOG BONE
LAKES
WILLOW
LAKE

MEADOW GATE

APPLE
ORCHARD

AGRICENTER
RESEARCH

AGRICENTER

VER

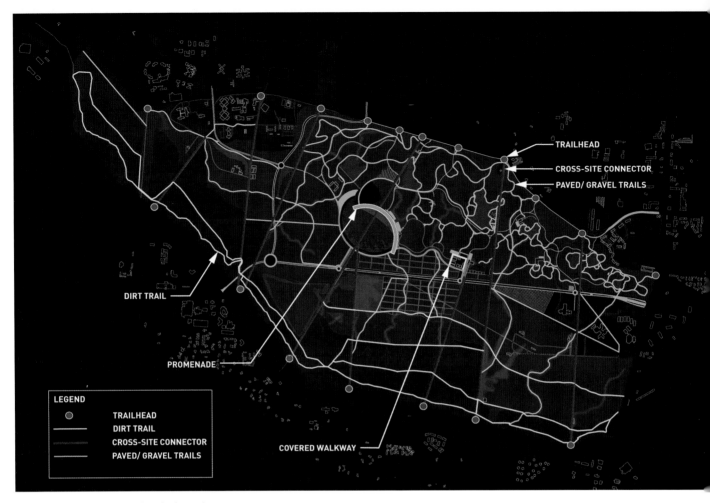

TRAILHEAD

CROSS-SITE CONNECTOR

PAVED/ GRAVEL TRAILS

DIRT TRAIL

PROMENADE

COVERED WALKWAY

LEGEND
- ⬤ TRAILHEAD
- —— DIRT TRAIL
- ······ CROSS-SITE CONNECTOR
- —— PAVED/ GRAVEL TRAILS

Site lines extend from the levees along the river and become both visual and physical connections within the park.

the design needed to physically embody that program—those were the two basic themes that we tried to mesh together. The physical aspect addressed orientation: We thought that it would be important for visitors to see a long distance across the park because it is such a large area and it is so difficult to know where you are in the park. When we visited the site, we walked along the levees perpendicular to the river, because that way we always knew we would eventually get to the river. It occurred to us that if the levees were articulated a bit, visitors would end up with a pretty good point of orientation, regardless of what landscape condition they might be moving through. Perhaps the lines of the levees could be extended even further upland all the way across the property and create a series of view lines and lines of movement that would open up areas and provide orientation for anyone moving across the grain of these lines.

That was the very abstract physical idea we had: we wanted to retain the view lines at a scale

resembling Versailles as a way to make the whole place physically and visually knowable—in the same way that at Versailles you occasionally see the whole site and understand the network in which you are operating. It's easier to understand and use the park when you can sense the whole.

The programmatic idea related to the fact that there was a lot of good farmland on the site—after all, the place had been a farm for a long time—but it didn't have anything to do with local organic or sustainable agriculture. We also learned that Memphis is known as the "heaviest city" in the United States, with the country's highest rates of obesity and Type 2 diabetes. We thought that a more progressive and potentially revenue-generating farm operation would be relevant here and perhaps of interest to the Agricenter. This farm could be shared with the Shelby Farms Conservancy, which had a more progressive agenda, and could be located right

JANUARY FEBRUARY MARCH APRIL MAY JUNE JULY AUGUST SEPTEMBER OCTOBER NOVEMBER DECEMBER

TOMATO
ASPARAGUS
BLACKBERRY
LEEK
SQUASH
CAULIFLOWER
BROCCOLI
PECAN
BROCCOLI
CABBAGE
EGGPLANT
CHERRY
KALE
CUCUMBER
KALE
ONION
BELL PEPPER
BLUEBERRY
SNAPBEAN

GOURDS

CARROT
GRAPE
LETTUCE
STRAWBERRY
IRISH POTATO
GREENS
GREENS
MUSHROOM
SWEET POTATO
RASPBERRY
SWEET POTATO
OKRA
PLUM
BOK CHOY
COLLARDS
GARLIC
FIELD PEA
APPLE
RHUBARB
SWEET CORN
PUMPKIN
SPINACH
PEAR
BEET
TURNIP
SNOW PEA
PEACH
WATERMELON

Top: The crop diagram organizes a productive landscape that can provide local food alternatives within the Memphis market.
Bottom: Farming is at the core of the proposal and property. The productive landscape becomes a place for community involvement, recreation, and job creation.

The proposal works on many levels to serve the community and region of Memphis.

in the center of the site, serving as the driving programmatic and economic factor within the park.

So the two most important elements of the scheme were the view lines as a structuring device and the organic farm as a program that indicated the park's mission and provided major revenue. Where the view lines cross the highway they would become a wide land bridge that would strongly connect the two sides. This would also allow the farm to exist on both sides of the road, so that both the conservancy and the Agricenter could share in its management and the revenue it generated. The farm itself could grow in fifty-acre increments over time up to around three hundred acres as the market expanded. Our economist identified that Memphis was a completely unexploited market for local organic food, which gave us the idea to initiate a whole new green industry that doesn't currently exist in Memphis. The proposal thus became more of an activist

program than a normal regional park. It set about to engineer some things that don't currently exist and that aren't usually part of regional parks, such as markets, food, and other economic drivers.

JK: **What percentage of the site is currently actively farmed and how is the rest of the property managed?**

TL: I think about 30 or 35 percent is farmed. The rest of it is just mowed. The conservancy doesn't have a large budget for operating the park, so the easiest and cheapest way to keep everything under control is to mow it. They actually still use prison labor to do that. The mowing, of course, creates a pretty sterile, non-diverse landscape, similar to a golf course.

JK: **Obviously, with such a large project, where and how to act is a crucial decision. How did you address those questions?**

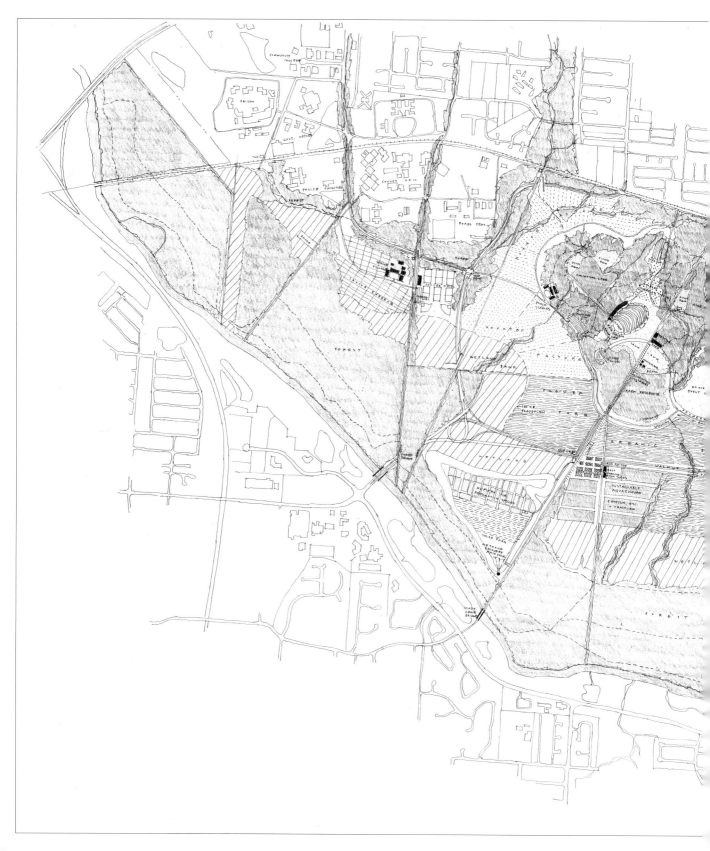

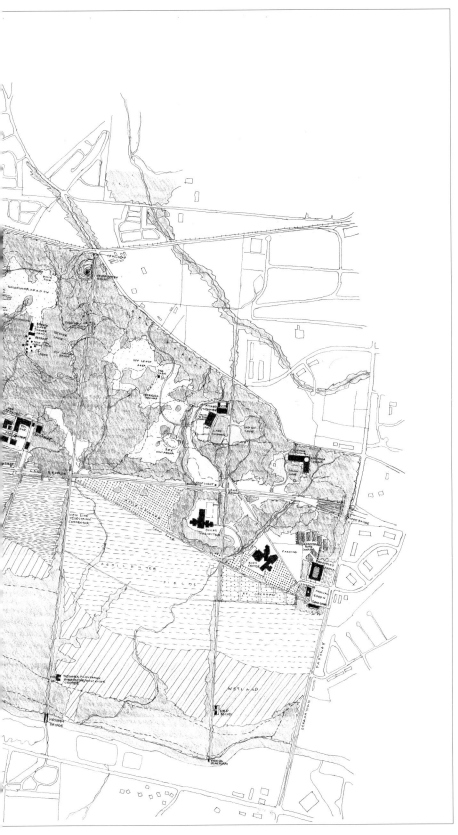

Top: The phasing diagram and aerial illustrate the incremental approach of the project.
Bottom: Alterations to the land and management techniques reactivate the site's natural ecological function.

SOIL & WATER: 2010

Restore Streams
Wetland Restoration / Mitigation Bank
Stream Planting
Forest Planting
Relocate Existing Programs
Trails
Roads + Utilities
Reservoir
Organic Farm to 25 acres
Event Green
Establish View Lines

HOMESTEAD & TRACTORS: 2012

Amphitheater + Rain Curtain
Restaurant + Market Hall
Hall of Flowers + Spillway Bridge
Catch'Em Lake + Sports Fields
Organic Farm to 50 acres
Transit Systems
2 Art Installations / Tower
Solar Farm

BARNS & GREENHOUSES: 2016

Farm Bridge / Meadow Bridge / Agricenter Bridge
3 Art Installations
Agricenter Arrival
Public Stables
Toddler Resort
Ecology Center
Dogbone Lake
Organic Farm to 75 acres
Observatory
Biomass Research Lab
Artist in Residence Gallery / Studio

FIELD EXPANSION: 2020

Fitness Center
Senior Village
4 Art Installations
Organic Farm to 125 acres
Neshoba Lodge
BMX

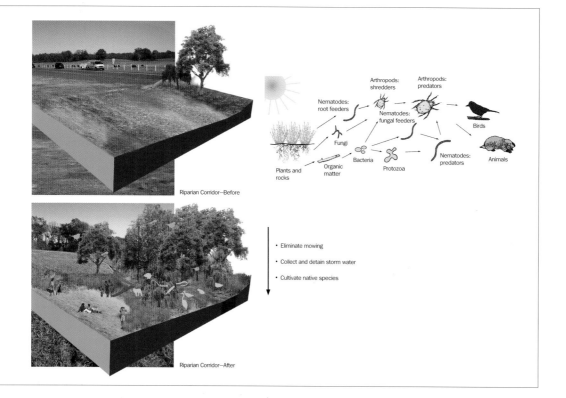

Riparian Corridor—Before

Riparian Corridor—After

Plants and rocks
Organic matter
Bacteria
Protozoa
Fungi
Nematodes: root feeders
Nematodes: fungal feeders
Nematodes: predators
Arthropods: shredders
Arthropods: predators
Birds
Animals

• Eliminate mowing

• Collect and detain storm water

• Cultivate native species

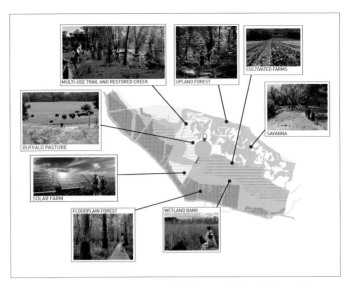

TL: After the first meeting with the jurors we came back with the idea of the view lines across the site, which intrigued people, but then we struggled for a way to address the site programmatically at this scale. For the second meeting I did a gigantic hand drawing that tried to map out everything, but it wasn't an impressive physical proposal. I remember hearing someone ask, "Where's the big idea?" Some of the other firms were proposing massive scale changes, but I never felt that we should just completely decimate or transform the place. It didn't need that and it wouldn't work anyway. There's just not enough capital to make that happen.

Finally, we realized our approach needed to be more incremental and be addressed in a farmlike manner to have a chance of working: We had to do things simply but with direct intentions. The first interventions needed to establish the framework to get started so that later developments could vary as much as they needed to. This approach was similar to the way a farmer goes out and plants a series of hedgerows or excavates an irrigation trench because he knows you need water and wind deflection before anything else is possible. That's how I saw it.

JK: At this scale any proposal had to consider the site from an ecological perspective. How did you see your proposal altering the ecology of the park?

TL: Clearly, a large part of the project was going to consist of regenerating and cultivating nature over the whole site. The way the site was being managed on both sides of the highway tended toward a lack of diversity resulting from all the mowing. In order to stimulate both farming and the growing of meadows, wetlands, and forests, the water system would need to be seriously re-worked, so that it could hold more water and not just drain it all off into the river. The road

Volunteers and green job trainees work as "farmers" to stimulate the site's active ecology.

also couldn't interrupt the water system from connecting ecologically down to the river. We wanted to reestablish stream corridors that could pass underneath the highway in the same way that the pedestrian corridors would pass over the top.

JK: **What are the realities of trying to implement a project of such scale and ambition?**

TL: If you want to retain more water and generate more diversity, you need a lot more management both in terms of agriculture and in terms of managing the forest and the park meadows and so forth. It occurred to us that one solution was to treat the park like a Works Progress Administration project instead of a normal regime of capital improvements where big contractors come out and do massive earthworks and everything gets done very

quickly. We thought that it would be better in this case to get a much larger group of people involved. Our idea was to employ a whole series of farmers to move forward incrementally, using many more people, even if they would be working for relatively low wages. The project would thus also be a way to do green job training, whether it be managing forests, running the farm, or operating normal concessions.

JK: **The scheme makes some very bold gestures across the landscape that without understanding the design intents may appear arbitrary. Did you simplify the project for the jury or general public to read themselves?**

TL: We used the image of a leaf to explain the scheme. Although it is simple, it did have a lot of meaning for us and symbolized our idea of interweaving the water and pedestrian site systems. The basic diagram of a very dense series of veins

The site's reconnected water system serves as the basis for dense networks of program. The image of a leaf is used to symbolize the networks and as a pattern for the roof of a hall of flowers, where visitors can experience a variety of flowers up close.

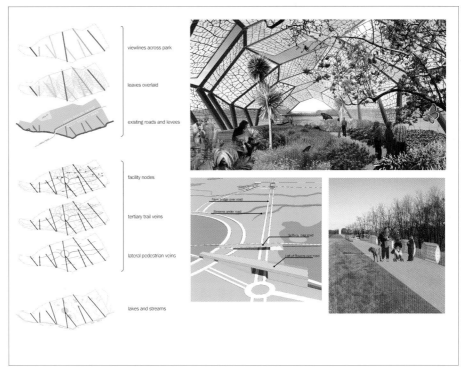

attached to a structural midrib clarified how these lines interacted with small-scale secondary and tertiary networks across the site as a way to structure use but also to allow diversity of program, nature, and species habitat.

JK: With any project of this size that is operating over such an extended period of time, I'm always curious about how the designer initiates the process of altering the landscape. What tools or elements did your proposal suggest to set the project in motion?

TL: The final proposal is essentially an earthwork and tree-clearing scheme to get a framework established that can be loaded with other program. But the water system is what has the most impact on the site's ecology and diversity. We knew that we needed a large reservoir to feed this farm. There was an existing lake close to the level of Walnut Grove Road, so we proposed to raise it up

to a higher level through earthworks and make it bigger. Gravity would then feed water to the large organic farm, which would emerge over time. From an experiential perspective, the reservoir would provide the recreational core of the project and function as a kind of arrival point. In order to communicate this function, we used the very obvious geometry of a circle for the lake and let some of the view lines pass across it.

JK: The program of the park is based on your efforts to make it self-sufficient economically. Is this interest an appropriate aim for a public park, and do you expect to see more projects developed in those terms?

TL: Yes, I think that's the way of the future. I think the days of huge donors are over, and there is going to be less and less direct public money for these kinds of projects. For better or worse the whole physical environment has to be able

Top: Gospel concert in the amphitheater

Bottom left: Beach at the reservoir and esplanade, with amphitheater beyond

Bottom right: Summer camp on Beaver Lake

In a way there are many very small moves that add up to a lot. Of course, there are also big implications in terms of how many people have to get involved to work the place.

JK: How was that approach or attitude received by the jury and by the public?

TL: We told people that they were going to be forest and stream managers and farmers rather than capital project managers. We felt it was important for everyone to grasp—and to embrace—that difference. That's also why we wanted to keep calling the site Shelby Farms Park. We weren't abandoning the farm's practices and principles; in fact, we were reusing them in a massive way. We always stressed to the jurors and the public that when you go to this place, you've got to get involved. In a certain way our approach is related to the Volkspark movement in northern Europe during the 1930s, which originated in an effort to improve public health. But in this case it takes more of a "pull-up-your-bootstraps" posture. It's a place that can help you. It's not without its institutional personality. It's not a faceless thing. You're going to encounter and deal with people when you go there a lot more than you're used to. At the same time you can still get lost in the cypress swamps.

I'm not sure whether everybody bought that idea. I think they were a bit scared about what would be involved organizationally. The conservancy and the Agricenter would have had to cooperate very directly and to really collaborate on the project.

JK: And they didn't cross that road so easily?

TL: They don't get along that well in general. I think one of the reasons why we didn't win the competition is because we pushed them pretty hard for that part of the project and for the physical

"Catch-em" lake: family catfish farm with barbecue barge

RACOON ART CONSTELLATION

ideas. We insisted that we should draw people from downtown, from outside the neighborhood, and balance rural and suburban values. We wanted to combine nature with elements that would be of interest to people who lived downtown such as music shows and carwashes, floating on barges and looking at art installations, and so forth. We felt we needed to add these types of things to the place if it was really going to be a park for the entire urban region of Memphis and not just another natural park preserve.

JK: **Given the scale of the property I would think including public art would be hard to see as an integral part of the park. When did you decide to include public art and how did the inclusion of art contribute to the scheme?**

TL: Actually, the park conservancy was interested in including art in the park; they commissioned Dennis Oppenheim and others to create projects

there. I think that part of the reason why we were selected to participate in the competition was because we had experience collaborating with artists. In our proposal we just took art as one of the crops we had to produce and felt that it could very easily be part of the program. How to include it was another question, but we soon realized that there was such a huge potential to distribute works across the property and to site them in a lot of different types of natural situations that we really ought to take advantage of the diversity of the site versus creating some localized art park tourist destination.

JK: **Would these works be part of a standing collection or would they be commissioned especially for the park?**

TL: The problem with much public art is that people feel alienated from it. They don't understand where it comes from and why it is

Observation tower overlooking the art "constellation"

there. So I proposed instead to establish a program where artists would be brought to the site for six months at a stretch. They would live there and then create a project on the site based on what they had observed about the place, what they had eaten, and whom they had met; they would also have a gallery there to show their work and give a couple of lectures. Both the visitors to the park and the artist would benefit from this interaction.

JK: **How would people navigate a 4,500-acre art gallery?**

TL: We wanted people to experience the installations in a similar way as in Janet Cardiff's audio walks, where you navigate some larger place using a CD and a pair of headphones. As people move through the park, they would come upon different pieces. At first we thought we should just propose that Janet do a piece. But then we realized it would be great for people to come upon a whole series of installations by different artists. The collection would grow over time, and projects would not be connected by any of the normal trails but instead by some other abstract network that would be navigated with a map and compass. In order to represent this idea of a network across the site we developed a constellation, or star chart, for the park that was shaped like a raccoon, Tennessee's state animal.

JK: **The proposal deals with a great number of issues and programmatic elements ranging from water infrastructure to sustainable energy, local food, and job creation. Is all that plus an artist-in-residence program too much?**

TL: Our main goal was to present a balance of emphasis. Even though nature would certainly dominate the park—80 percent of all land mass would consist of a natural landscape that would be brought back close to a primeval state—we also

Left: Approach to the observation tower designed by Coleman Coker
Right: Site installation concept by Coleman Coker

wanted to respond to people who would be more interested in music or food or in stuff for kids or in art. We wanted very much to treat them equally as constituencies. So the decision we made was not to position the park as a giant ecological preserve with a few recreational fields and outbuildings but as an urban park, and the idea of cultivating all these elements was the key to that.

Railroad Park

Birmingham, Alabama

The Birmingham Railroad Park serves as the central project in the revitalization of the Railroad Reservation area of downtown Birmingham. The design proposal uses the simple means of topography to manage stormwater, circulation, and small- and large-scale public events. Situated between two historic steel furnaces and bordered by a rail corridor that still activates the city, the park is an integral part of the master plan for the area and a dynamic new urban space that will feature urban trail connections, an amphitheater complex, a restaurant, and market spaces. Project currently under construction.

JK: **What is the history of this site?**

TL: Birmingham was originally a steel town that experienced its first real growth during the Civil War (before then most steel had been supplied by the North). There were two big steel furnaces—the Sloss Furnace and the Alyce Furnace—on either side of town, connected by railroad. During the Civil War, the city grew fairly quickly, and because there was so much traffic on the railroad, it eventually became difficult for people to cross from one side to the other. Therefore, in the early 1900s, the city planned, and in the 1920s built, a large viaduct through the center of town that allowed people to drive underneath the railway, which in this area was elevated by about fifteen feet. This portion of town encompassed about five or six blocks next to a big steam plant as well as a four-block zone known as the Railroad Reservation District, which consisted of warehousing and railroad spurs. As a result, the main part of downtown, which was north, became separated from the southern part of town, both by the viaduct and by this zone of many blocks that had become vacant as industry left the city limits. So for a very long time the city was divided into two areas.

Although unified as an open lot, the property has numerous property divisions and infrastructural easements that impact its development.

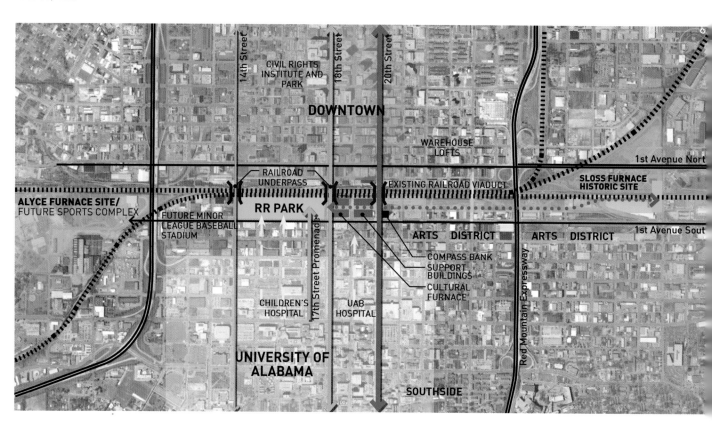

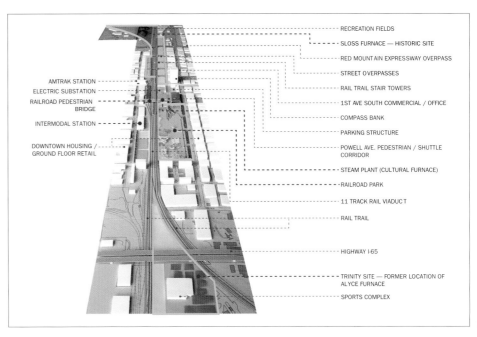

RECREATION FIELDS
SLOSS FURNACE — HISTORIC SITE
RED MOUNTAIN EXPRESSWAY OVERPASS
STREET OVERPASSES
RAIL TRAIL STAIR TOWERS
1ST AVE SOUTH COMMERCIAL / OFFICE
COMPASS BANK
PARKING STRUCTURE
POWELL AVE. PEDESTRIAN / SHUTTLE CORRIDOR
STEAM PLANT (CULTURAL FURNACE)
RAILROAD PARK
11 TRACK RAIL VIADUCT
RAIL TRAIL
HIGHWAY I-65
TRINITY SITE — FORMER LOCATION OF ALYCE FURNACE
SPORTS COMPLEX

AMTRAK STATION
ELECTRIC SUBSTATION
RAILROAD PEDESTRIAN BRIDGE
INTERMODAL STATION
DOWNTOWN HOUSING / GROUND FLOOR RETAIL

The park project is the centerpiece to the redevelopment master plan of the city's Railroad Reservation District.

JK: **When did the city decide to deal with this problem and how did you get involved?**

TL: The city had been studying the Railroad Reservation District for some time with different groups of consultants and advisors. Bill Gilchrist, Birmingham's director of planning and engineering, had involved groups from the American Institute of Architects and the Urban Land Institute in different planning studies. He even facilitated a Mayor's Institute on Birmingham that grew out of one of the Urban Land Institute's studies and looked at the railroad site specifically.

At first he just wanted me to come down on a per diem basis and talk to everyone involved about how to run a competition. At the time we had just finished losing a competition—one of the many we lost. So the first thing I insisted on was, "You *really* don't want to run a competition. It's going to be a disaster." I managed to persuade

the city of that and was asked to instead propose a master plan for the park and the surrounding district. After making some initial models and studies of the larger area, we gradually moved into what would be the general strategy for the park by thinking about how it could influence the larger area.

JK: **Was development already happening in the area or was the park seen as a development generator?**

TL: The idea to take the four blocks of the Railroad Reservation District, as it was called, and transform them into a public park originated during the master plan phase. The park would serve to bridge the north and south parts of downtown and function as a core amenity for the office, retail, and housing development that would happen throughout the area. The park itself would help stimulate a lot of that development,

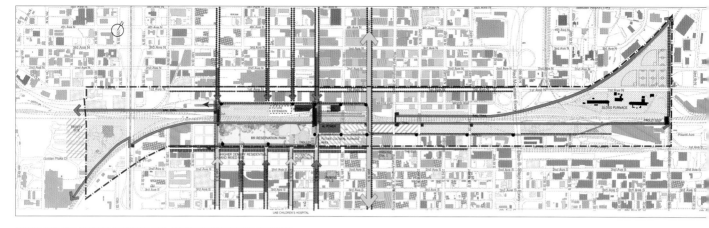

Master plan. The proposal facilitates east–west pedestrian and recreational connections between the existing furnace sites. The park itself is located at the northern terminus of five city streets.

so it was definitely seen as the city's key project, a real linchpin for the urban redevelopment of Birmingham.

JK: **How have the development and the project been impacted by the recent economic crisis?**

TL: While some commercial development has certainly slowed down, private development is still happening. Many people are converting warehouses to lofts, and the area is starting to have a more urban lifestyle and to be a more integrated part of the city. The park is still very much going to be at the center of all that.

JK: **How much interaction did you have with the general public as the master plan was being developed?**

TL: Renee Kemp-Rotan, the project manager assigned by the mayor's office, set up a massive public outreach effort. We had meetings from 7 in the morning until 7 at night with every interest group and stakeholder under the sun and many, many presentations. It was totally exhausting. I had never been through anything like it. I met so many people that often, when I see them now, I have to confess they look familiar but I can't remember from where.

We spent a good four or five months making presentations of our district model to everybody you could think of. It was only toward the end of the public process that we began to condense everything into a program that still guides us. But as a result of those efforts, the project was exceptionally well grounded in the city's residents and we ended up with a design that spoke of railway plus a community plus nature.

JK: **What elements of the larger area influenced your ambitions for the park site?**

Gateway plaza at Seventeenth Street

TL: We looked at the whole zone from the old Alyce Furnace site up to the Sloss Furnace. The Sloss Furnace is a national historic landmark and now serves as the venue for heavy metal concerts. It is an important tourist destination in Birmingham, so one of our goals was to connect the park with it. We proposed a rail trail and a trolley system from the park to Sloss Furnace so people could easily move back and forth and also access the intermodal station, which is directly across the rail viaduct from the park at Eighteenth Street.

Another important consideration was the fact that the park site was so strongly connected to the urban grid. Five streets touch the park: Fourteenth and Eighteenth streets run along its eastern and western edges, and Fifteenth, Sixteenth, and Seventeenth streets all dead-end right on the south side of the park. This meant that there needed to be multiple entries on the south side and it

suggested a certain way of subdividing the park longitudinally.

We decided to create gateway plazas at each of the streets that intersect the park blocks, all based on the urban grid and with the idea that they would draw a fair amount of retail activity and create a populated corridor that would feed directly into the park. This idea also allowed us to break the park down into structured zones that can be used separately or combined as one larger open space.

By far the largest issue we had to deal with, however, was that somehow this park was supposed to bridge the north and south areas of downtown. I kept thinking to myself, "I don't understand how we can accomplish that." Initially, I was thinking about it in a far too literal way, "Are we going to make a tunnel in the viaduct? Is the city going to get rid of the railroad? Can we bridge it over?" Of course, all of those things are very difficult and expensive to do and take up a lot

Top: A trail along the rail corridor establishes an east–west pedestrian connection from the Sloss Furnace to the park and facilitates the community's hobby of trainspotting.

Bottom: The scheme features an extensive re-contouring of the site that structures the park's public use. At its southern edge gateway plazas lead into the park.

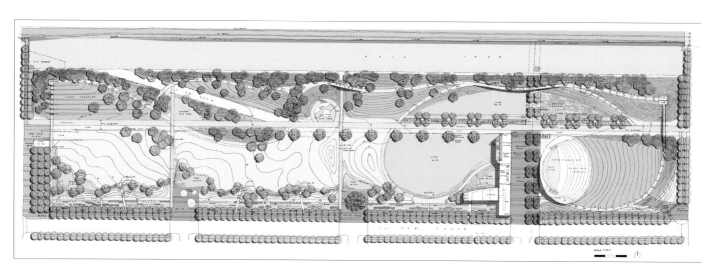

of room. Gradually, it became clear to me that since the city liked the railroad so much anyway and didn't want to subjugate or remove it, the only way to respond to it was to honor it, to let people have some direct experience with the trains.

So one of the first key issues was to find a way to let people circulate and experience the trains up at the level of the railway, instead of down within the park. We also wanted to provide a larger physical and visual space for the trains and create reflecting pools for them, so that the railway actually became the most dynamic area of the site. The city liked the idea of letting the public experience the railway at the level of the trains or even above them. This also provided people with an overview of the space on the other side of town and the park itself and thus helped to link the two parts of the city. We created a rail trail, which consists of both an on-grade walkway on top of small hills and of elevated walkways that connect the hills. This rail trail really helps visitors understand what the place is about and where it came from.

JK: **Usually, you see communities looking to remove or repurpose their existing rails when industrial areas of town are redeveloped. What was it about the railroad that the community liked so much?**

TL: In a lot of cities the train skirts the edge of town or separates the city from the water or is just some kind of abandoned scar. In Birmingham it is still very busy. There are eleven tracks that are all active. People here really like the train. It's their main regional orientation device. There's no bay, there's no river, no large-scale natural element, so the city is still oriented to the railway and it even becomes a pastime. People do train spotting on the weekend from some of the overpass bridges further down the line.

The existing viaduct is raised some fifteen feet above the park.
Early proposals used both the topography and structure to bring
visitors up to and above the rail corridor.

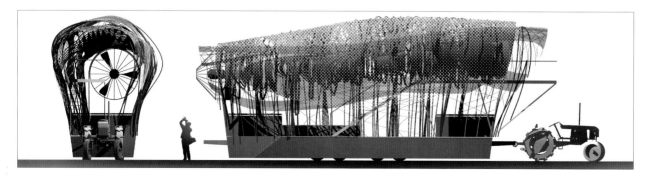

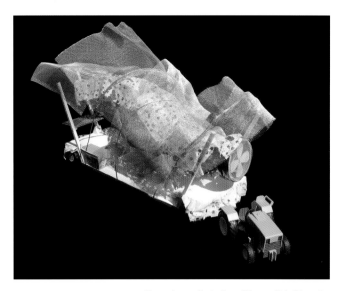

Top and opposite bottom: "Bivouac Baby" is an ice cream truck proposed to slowly traverse the park's central promenade.

JK: **Working along highway and rail corridors always has its hurdles—with utilities and easements. What challenges has that situation presented to the project and how have you responded as the park develops?**

TL: One of the problems we encountered was that a lot of the land to the east of the park site is still owned by the shipping and transportation company Norfolk Southern. Norfolk Southern doesn't want to give up any of their land so that has complicated our idea of developing park corridors and gateway plazas. The first order of business is to make the park work as well as it possibly can given all the restrictions we discovered. As we learned more about the problematic ownerships in adjacent areas, we proposed to use the one existing right-of-way street, Powell Avenue, which bisects the site, as the spine that can connect whatever parcels become available later and can link the park

with Sloss Furnace. We are now developing a vehicle that is also an art installation, which will serve as a trolley within the park and to Sloss Furnace.

JK: **Beyond facilitating pedestrian connections through the park and along the railroad, what other program did the park have to respond to?**

TL: One thing the community required was a large open space for festivals. There are two each year: the Southern Heritage Festival and the Crawfish Boil, where there is food, music, and up to forty thousand people in one spot. In addition, the park was to allow for smaller, more frequent events such as various performances or markets spread throughout the park.

JK: **How does the proposal respond to such a varied program?**

Top: Annual Crawfish Boil
Middle and Bottom: The park will feature amenities including a restaurant, open-air market, large amphitheater, and shaded promenade that allow it to be a place of rest during the day and the center of activity at night.

TL: The basic diagram of the project always had more articulated edges, while the center was left largely open so that it could be used for festivals and by the surrounding neighborhood. However, I was worried that there would be too many amenities distributed along the southern edge, where all the retail and housing would be and where pedestrians accessed the park. If we didn't draw people deep into the park all the way across to the other side, the middle would become a dead zone, with the accompanying maintenance and security problems. To me that issue was one of the most important parts of the project. We decided to drag the rail trail, the range of small hills, the stream at their base, other water features, and elements of architectural interest such as an amphitheater and small stages carved into the hillsides over to the north side and let the foreground be more of an open space.

JK: **Looking at both the initial and final schemes, it is obvious that topography was extensively altered to facilitate program and define a structure for the park. How did you change the site from its previous condition?**

TL: The area had once been a marsh and the lowest point in the city, but the entire site had been filled as industry grew and the railroad flourished. We decided early on to make use of the larger watershed and collect as much water as we could and funnel it into a storage facility, which would become a lake or a reservoir at the high end of the site. From this reservoir, water would descend through a system of streams and ponds and finally reenter Village Creek, which is connected to the west end of the park.

Having a reservoir served two purposes: it introduced a natural feature right next to the railroad and it became an important element in the city's stormwater system. There is frequent

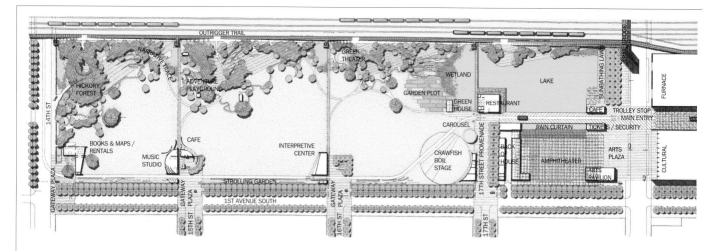

Master plan. Street grid strongly expressed, very direct connection to potential Cultural Furnace site across Eighteenth Street, contingent on early construction of that project.

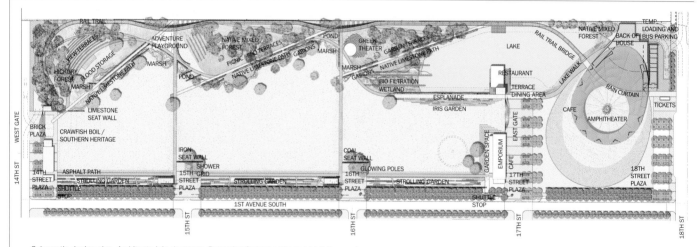

Schematic design plan. Architects join the team. Departing from the street grid–influenced master plan, the amphitheater took a freer form, with a large retractable fabric canopy and better servicing. Pavilions at each entry plaza are exchanged for East Gate and West Gate structures, which are established as gateways to the cavernous open space.

As plans have evolved, the basic structure of the scheme has allowed it to respond to the changing programmatic needs, construction limitations, and economic conditions.

The proposal uses topography as the major design tool to structure the park's relationship to its context, including the elevated rail viaduct, and to manage hydrology by collecting and treating stormwater.

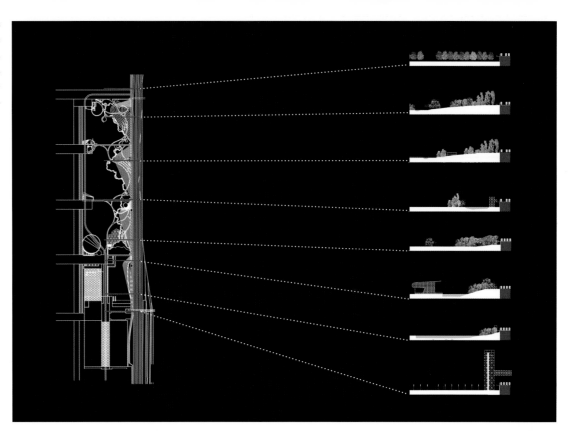

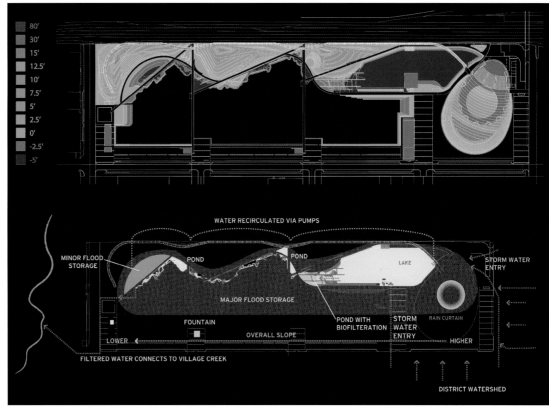

80'
30'
15'
12.5'
10'
7.5'
5'
2.5'
0'
-2.5'
-5'

WATER RECIRCULATED VIA PUMPS

MINOR FLOOD STORAGE

POND

POND

LAKE

STORM WATER ENTRY

MAJOR FLOOD STORAGE

POND WITH BIOFILTERATION

STORM WATER ENTRY

RAIN CURTAIN

FOUNTAIN

LOWER

OVERALL SLOPE

HIGHER

FILTERED WATER CONNECTS TO VILLAGE CREEK

DISTRICT WATERSHED

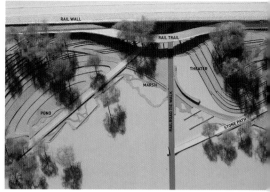

Left: Early rendering of the lake and rail trail
Right: Elevated and at-grade paths connect through the park, providing for alternative and varied means of travel through the city.

flooding from torrential rains during hurricane season in Birmingham, so it helps to have a place for the water to gather, from where it can leak out slowly over time. In the end the reservoir was moved to the south instead of the north side of the park due to the rail and land ownership issues.

JK: **Did moving the reservoir change the way you were using the water on site?**

TL: No, the idea remained the same. In our work we always try to channel water and use it as a way to organize space, because it is an automatically sustainable element that serves to grow landscape. Wherever you concentrate water, you get growth of vegetation.

The topography of the park is structured in a way that each block is subdivided by a crossing boardwalk, which is an extension of the streets that end on the park. This is also where

the topography steps down as you move across the park from east to west. This terracing of the site enabled us to store stormwater at each level. Water descends over a series of weirs, so as a result there's a pond attached to each entry plaza. The boardwalks that extend from the entry plazas cross the weirs and lead to the rail trail. In addition there's a whole series of smaller ponds and weirs within each level of the park. So there's quite a bit of water storage there.

JK: **What percentage of the site does the water system occupy?**

TL: The stormwater system covers about 30 percent or more. Beside the reservoir and ponds there are areas of wetlands and wetter areas of plantings. Along most of the site there is a gradient from low, wet areas to dry, upland areas.

Left: Axonometric

Right: A major element within the design, the water system provides much needed flood control but also activates the ecology, recreation, and spectacle of the site.

JK: **Was the rail ownership issue the only physical constraint that caused the scheme to change?**

TL: No. Powell Street, which runs through the middle of the park, had a fifty-foot-wide rail easement that we had to deal with. Part of that easement contains a major electrical line that limited what we could do, but we managed to build the pedestrian walkway on top of the electric line. There's also another rail easement zone between the two lakes on the final plan, which has been reconstructed as a causeway. Part of the park to the north included another electric line easement, which will become a pedestrian garden along the two lakes with a series of rectangular islands that project into the southern lake.

JK: **Was soil contamination an issue given the site's historic use and proximity to the rail lines?**

TL: There was one hot spot where the groundwater was polluted below a certain level, so one of the lakes had to have a PVC liner underneath it to prevent any intrusion. Thankfully, the rest of the site has only low-level issues you normally find under urban sites. All we have to do is put a twelve-inch cap of topsoil over everything as long as we keep the soil on site and don't take it off. So it's a pretty clean site considering its history.

JK: **In view of both the public review process and the issues related to the site itself, how has the project maintained its legibility from initial concept to final plan as construction begins?**

TL: You always have to address change within the course of developing a project. In our work we aim to structure the design in a way that can survive throughout that process. In this case the use of the

Left: Rain Curtain at the retractable canopy
Right: Afternoon concert at the amphitheater

with the rail trail, which had to be there from the beginning.

As we moved into construction planning, the client decided to hire architects for both the amphitheater and the restaurant and market. HKW in Birmingham was hired in collaboration with KVA to design and document the amphitheater, while GA Studio in Birmingham was commissioned to design the restaurant and market.

As work went forward, we had to make huge changes to the plan due to utility discoveries. Eventually, we ran out of room for the amphitheater in its original position near the railroad and relocated it facing the plaza in a tighter arrangement with the restaurant and market.

The budget and the economy also had a big impact on these structures. The original amphitheater with the retractable roof had to be scaled back. The new scheme is an angled

cubist geometry in wood and perforated metal. The proscenium creates a large open arch, which provides a view through the theater when it's not in use for an event. The restaurant on the plaza was also scaled back. With the economic downturn, the original plan by GA for a Tavern on the Green–type of facility done in Corten steel had to become something much simpler that would still allow food service and market space under cover but out of doors. Tom Leader Studio has now become the design architect for that scheme, because it's such an outdoor piece. The design is based on the idea of a series of wooden boxcars that sit next to the plaza and are covered by a very simple large metal train shed–type canopy that extends the entire length of the plaza. We called the structure East Gate because it serves as a major threshold to the lake and open space to the west, as well as framing views back to the amphitheater entry and porch.

Site grading in process, summer 2009

JK: **The project is currently in construction. What stage is it in and when will it be finished?**

TL: Right now the site has been rough-graded so you can really see the effect of the topography. This fall the major hardscape, stream, and lake work will be done and then planting and irrigation will begin in early spring 2010. The East Gate structure and the rail trail will be completed by late spring so the big opening is planned for May or June of 2010.

Pool Pavilion Forest

Napa Valley, California

Pool Pavilion Forest, completed in 2007, was a collaboration between artist James Turrell, Tom Leader, and architect Jim Jennings. The project consists of two Turrell Sky Spaces: one situated in a new swimming pool and the other in a new entertainment pavilion. This complex accompanied the construction of an art cave, designed by Bade Stageberg Cox, that was commissioned by the clients, art collectors Norah and Norman Stone, to display some of the oversized art works they had purchased over the years. The topography of the sixteen-acre site with rolling hills was dramatically altered to create a unified composition while preserving the most essential landscape features of forest, vineyard, and existing farmhouse.

JK: **How did you get involved with this project?**

TL: The first time I met the clients, Norah and Norman Stone, was while I was still working for Peter Walker. Aaron Betsky, who was the curator of architecture at San Francisco's Museum of Modern Art at the time, mentioned my name when the Stones had commissioned Thom Mayne to design a winery for the site and needed a landscape architect. Mayne had taken the scheme far enough to get an estimate, but there was a big budget problem. In the end the project had to be abandoned. When we met, Norman and I had a great conversation about his vineyard and the idea of cultivation, of trying to make something out of the landscape that was more fundamental than usual and went beyond the decorative. Norman was quite taken with that.

In late 2001 or early 2002 he approached me with a new project: the Stones had commissioned a Sky Space by James Turrell that was to be located inside a swimming pool, and they needed a landscape architect to design the site. I think Aaron and curator Leah Levy had recommended me. Norman called me one day out of the blue and said, "Tom, do you remember me?

Top: View of the site from the existing farm house.

Bottom and opposite: The existing site was developed mostly as a vineyard and featured large stands of redwood trees along the slope to the south.

We've commissioned James Turrell to do a piece for us and we'd like it to be inside a swimming pool—you swim into it from under water. We're looking for some help with that. Would you like to come up and take a look?" Obviously, I said yes.

Philippe Coignet, then an associate at Tom Leader Studio, and I drove up to the site for a meeting with Norman and Norah. We presented a slender volume of our work, which included competitions, experimental projects, and installations. It must have had a pulse that resonated, because Norman only said, "Fine, let's get started"—just like that. At the time the project was still at the very beginning. The Stones had commissioned Turrell and had had a conversation with him about what they wanted to do, but he didn't have a sense of how to site the piece itself and thought they needed a site designer.

JK: Did the Stones already have the property?

TL: They had owned this property for quite a while, at least ten years I think, and used it for parties, holidays, and to display some temporary and permanent art installations. Most of the site, which was about sixteen acres altogether, was used to grow grapes for wine making. The Stones were very interested in producing world class Merlot, so the vineyards on the site were precious to them. They didn't want the project to impinge on the grapes, so the scheme needed to be very compact.

JK: **Having to deal with a site that is restricted by existing uses is a difficult starting point for a project. How did you approach the site in your initial schemes and how were these early schemes received by the clients?**

TL: At the beginning my main goal was to find a way to take on the whole place rather than just designing a pool and situating a sculpture. I thought the design needed to engage the site very

Steep terraces on the south slope are remnants of the property's previous use and were once planted with a prune orchard.

fundamentally to take the best advantage of it. It was a pretty interesting site, but it had some messy parts as well. The existing property had a random arrangement of swimming pool, garage, and driveway, which were all partly hidden by shrubs and trees. It was a site that was hard to read. We knew that we had to clean things up and provide more order and that a larger part of the site had to be addressed.

The starting point of our work, however, was to decide where the pool should go; that was the first order of business. The initial scheme was the most compact siting we could possibly figure out, with the pool jammed up fairly close to the house. It wasn't very successful, and the Stones didn't like it either.

The next design we considered took on much more of the site. There were several existing terraces on the south side of the property, which had been logged about one hundred years before. The owner at the time had planted a prune

orchard on the terraces, but since then they had been left alone, and a general native forest of firs and maples had regrown. All that was left of the orchard were the terraces with very steep slopes in between. It was hard to even climb up there. We thought that the terraces were a pretty interesting place for an outdoor sculpture gallery. From that initial idea we developed the shape of an arc that followed the terraces and the base of the slope and continued to curve all the way around an existing grove of redwood trees out toward the house. It was an interesting idea, but it tried too hard to pick up on the hillside terraces, repeating them as an organizing move out toward the house and the landscape and extending them into an arc that would also form the access road. I don't think the Stones liked this idea very much either.

JK: **So neither extreme—compact or grand— worked for either one of you; what was it that finally clarified the direction of the scheme?**

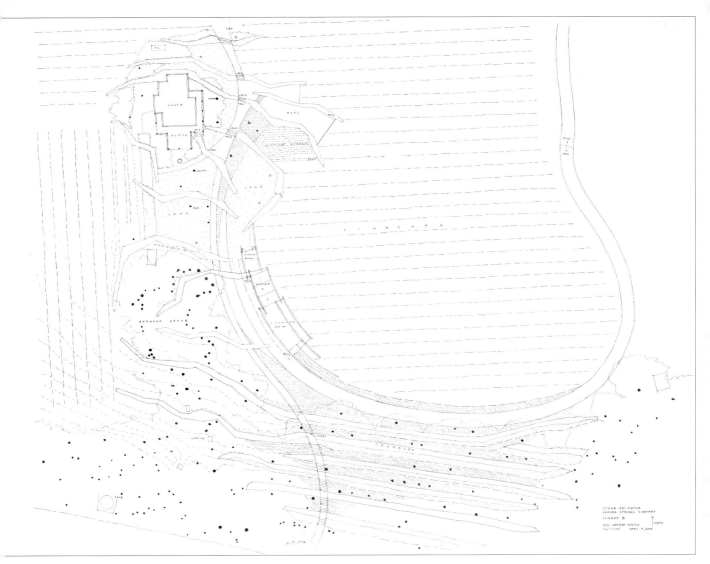

Early curving site plan, later abandoned

 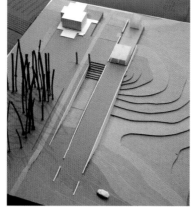 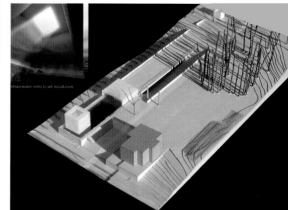

Left: Early schemes kept all of the elements densely packed into a linear bar called the "land bridge," in order to keep the development compact and preserve the existing vineyards as much as possible.
Middle and right: Early models of the land bridge with Sky Space and pool pavilion

TL: In the course of our conversations with the clients about the pool the program expanded to include changing rooms and an outdoor dining area, along with enough space for the Stones to entertain. They hold large parties, and they are well known socially. Norah wanted a really big flat lawn. The existing lawn was too lumpy, and people were always twisting their ankles. The Stones thought the changing rooms should be near the pool but tucked behind some trees or located someplace else. We started by looking at it that way, but didn't like the idea of people having to run across the lawn in their swimsuits to get to the pool, so these additional elements began to attach themselves to the pool. Eventually, it became clear that there would be one general assembly of structures consisting of the changing rooms and dining facilities, some shading for that, and the pool with the Sky Space. But how do you arrange all these elements? One day, it just seemed obvious to

try lining everything up and extending out from the base of the hillside.

JK: **That idea feels much more like one layered onto the site rather than one generated from it.**

TL: Yes. I actually resisted for a long time to line up the elements, because that scheme felt a lot like the work I had been doing for the past fifteen to twenty years with Peter Walker. I was looking for something more idiosyncratic or site-generated, but I finally realized that it's okay. The design is in fact site-generated in that it makes a very clear and direct connection with the base of the hill, tying everything together into one piece. It was also the most direct, flattering move related to the redwood trees on the hillside. The scheme could almost be compared to a redwood tree that had fallen down to the north. These trees are so tall and linear that having this complimentary line, which runs horizontally instead of vertically, just felt right.

Left: This early design sketch shows how the land bridge is seen as an extension of the hillside and the stand of redwood trees.
Right: Early modeling experiment

By the time we developed the first early sketch model, the design had evolved into a clear land bridge: a bridge of land that extended from the base of the hill as a flat plane and was free from the undulation of the surrounding topography. The fact that it passes right along the very edge of the redwood grove anchors the design to the trees very strongly.

JK: **Did lining elements up to form the land bridge create any issues that you had to address?**

TL: The scheme did a lot to clarify the site but it was difficult to integrate a garage, as there were already too many outbuildings. It was very cluttered. The first solution we came up with was to put the garage underground, underneath the land bridge, accessed via a steep ramp. This deep hole in the ground had an interesting three-dimensional aspect to it, but it came with its own set of problems: the need for an elevator, having

to put the landscape on top of the garage, and the expense. But because we were trying to conserve the grapes as much as possible, this solution seemed the best one for quite a while.

JK: **Beyond aligning and even stacking the elements, how did you site each component within the linear scheme?**

TL: A very important part was a pair of level walls that would connect the entire design to the base of the hill and contain all its key elements—a lavender garden, the pavilion, and finally the pool with Turrell's Sky Space. Visitors would drive down the ramp behind these walls to access the garage. The three-dimensionality of the land bridge was much more apparent in this early scheme than in the final solution, because the two walls revealed much taller profiles (twelve to fifteen feet). The two walls remained an important part of the design but eventually became seat height.

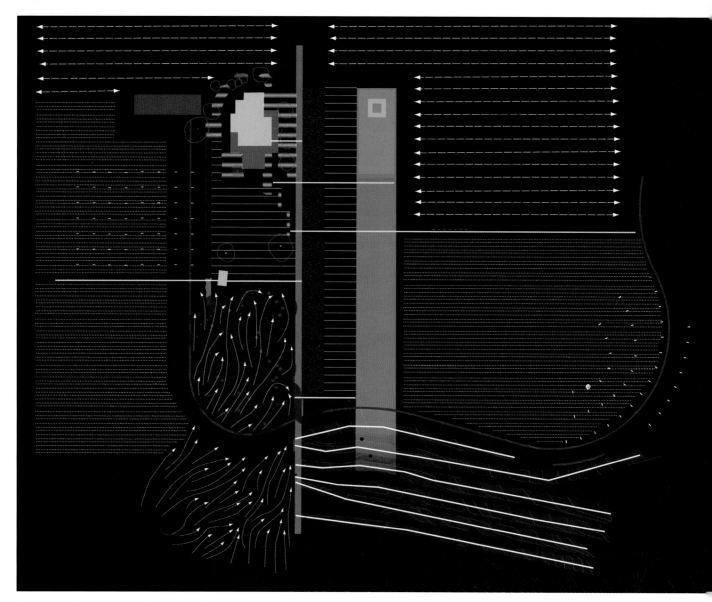

This conceptual diagram illustrates the geometry of
the site's elements—vineyards, redwoods, topography;
the dynamics of water and air moving across the site
are reflected in the order and structure of the built
elements.

The changing rooms and dining pavilion were located beyond the lavender garden, followed by the pool, with the Turrell piece located in the exalted position at the end of the pool. It was all one level assembly that gradually lifted out of the ground by seven feet at its culmination. It seemed logical to place the Sky Space at the end of this big tongue that extended from the hillside. In fact, it is a bit of an odd placement for Turrell, because most of his works of this nature are smaller and very discrete internal experiences rather than strong objects in space; in this case, however, it was very clearly a piece that needed to be floating on the water. I thought about it in comparison to—and I know this is kind of an absurd comparison—the fountain of Latona at Versailles. The fountain faces this great, grand axis and gestures out to the universe. In a way that is what the Sky Space is doing here, except it is oriented completely inward as a piece of art, so the design

had a little perversity to it, which I thought was interesting.

JK: **How did the client and Turrell respond to the scheme?**

TL: First we showed Norman a simple little model; he liked the idea of the land bridge right away and thought it would be great. He was excited and wanted to run it by Turrell, so we set up a meeting and went to see him fairly quickly. I had concerns about how he would receive such a forceful scheme.

JK: **Why were you worried?**

TL: Our design was axial and as such a pretty strong statement. You were either going to like it or not. It was quite different from the siting of a lot of Turrell's other works. But the meeting went well. I think both Norman and Turrell thought the

Three-dimensional study of the Sky Space's
underwater entry

design was logical. It dealt with the functional part of the project, and while I wouldn't call it land art, it certainly structured the site in a way that went beyond what was necessary. It made more out of the pool pavilion and the garden behind it and the attachment to the hill. The scheme was clear and direct. It allowed for the art to take place without the organization getting in the way. Typically, you don't want an art or sculpture garden to have too many particular and idiosyncratic elements that distract from the art itself.

JK: How did the scheme evolve from that first meeting?

TL: At that point the biggest change we made was to the pavilion with the changing rooms. Our initial idea had been to make a single structure that included both the Sky Space and men's and women's changing rooms. This structure would cover the width of the entire land bridge and would cantilever over the edge of the pool, so that the pool would actually come inside the space. People would use the changing rooms and then dive into the water from inside the building, like James Bond. That was what we showed in our first model, but Turrell and the client were less convinced about that part. Turrell suggested to instead create a second work of light art that was separate from the Sky Space in the pool in order to accommodate the necessary uses related to the pool and entertaining. He proposed building a four-corner pavilion that would be open on all the cardinal points. This pavilion would include independent structures for changing and food preparation and would support another plane overhead with a second Sky Space oculus that could be easily lit from the top of the smaller independent structures.

We worked with that idea for a while, but it was troublesome from the start. All the small structures made things cluttered and the scheme was also quite expensive. At that point everyone agreed we ought to ask an architect to join our team, so I invited Jim Jennings to work with us.

JK: **Had you worked with Jennings before?**

TL: I had never worked with him but he seemed like the perfect person to join the team because a lot of his work is very similar to what the project was starting to become—a fairly stripped down and planar extrusive scheme. Everyone agreed Jim would be a good match, and he was interested and liked the design, which was important. He wanted to get involved without needing to start over. He was the perfect collaborator in an unusual situation where the architect comes in later than the landscape architect. Things usually happen the other way around.

JK: **How did the three of you work together?**

TL: We got along very well and became friends and supported each other through the whole process. I think Turrell felt very comfortable because Jim's office is technically strong, so he was confident they could figure out the Sky Spaces in detail. Jim's office really knows how to build things—creating perfect concrete, perfect metal surfaces—and Paul Endres, who was doing structural work for Jim at the time, is very creative and has a tensile approach to things, which was important with the idea that Jim eventually came up with.

Jim's thought was—and we agreed—that it would be preferable not to block the extension of the space by the pavilion Turrell had proposed. His idea was to instead build a bar structure containing the changing room and a small kitchen and move it to the left of the view, parallel to the axis. A plane, which would cantilever over the entire space would then sit on very slender columns. This simple overhead plane would define the pavilion and become the second Sky Space. That, of course,

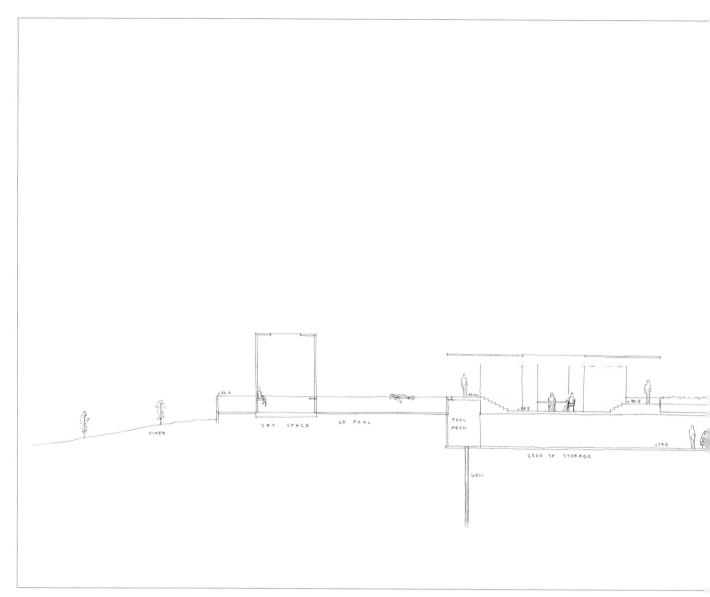

VINES

SKY SPACE

60' POOL

+ 92.0

POOL
MECH.

WELL

+ 92.0

+ 88.5

+ 90.5

+ 79.5

2300 SF STORAGE

Longitudunal section through early Turrell idea for pavilion

LAVENDER GARDEN

RKING

90.5
ENTRY ROAD

+96
PATH TO
LOG INSTALLATION

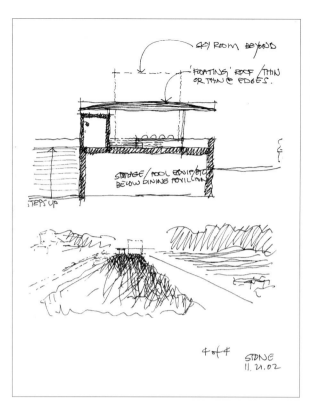

is the design we ended up with. The only problem with this scheme was that it was impossible to light the overhead plane evenly from only one side. The lights all have to be located at exactly the same distance from the surface overhead, have the same wattage, and come from the same type of lamp in order to provide absolutely even lighting. Turrell, of course, is very particular about achieving a perfect illumination of the surface.

JK: **The surface of the pool creates another perfect plane; was it seen as related to the overhead planes of the two Sky Spaces?**

TL: The pool itself was always supposed to be part of the general extrusion from the ground, as part of the land bridge, but we wanted it to have a precise visual connection to the house and pavilion area. We worked with Turrell to figure out its exact elevation. We wanted the level of the pool surface to relate to the sightlines from the house to the top of the vineyard posts.

Eventually, we determined a single datum for the extrusion, which was at elevation 90.5 feet for the level of the surface paving and 92 feet for the top of the walls. That datum was perfectly observed throughout the entire length of the land bridge. The water of the pool is not flush with the paving but at the higher 92-foot datum. This subtle difference decreases the angle at which you're viewing the water, so you get a much stronger reflection off of it. If you're looking down at the pool, it's easy for your eye to go straight into the water. Turrell wanted to keep the pool surface as close as possible to people's eye level, so it was determined that the water level would be kept flush with the walls. We created this "knife-edge" condition by using flat granite that could be cut to a precise line, so that there is water subtly overflowing on all sides, creating so-called "wet edges." This results

Top: The pavilion ceiling
Bottom: Rendering of the pool with pavilion
and second Sky Space

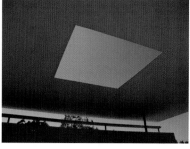

Left: Vineyard and oak groves beyond

Right: Details of Sky Space with light troughs

JK: **How is the overhead plane illuminated?**

TL: In the initial scheme Turrell's idea had been to light the Sky Space from the roofs of each of the four structures he had first proposed, and it would have been easy to install the lights at the same distance. In the new design, however, there was only the top of the bar structure on the west side and nothing on the east side except the slender columns supporting the roof. We considered installing the lights in the seat walls, but they would probably have burned people's bottoms if they sat on them, and the glare would have been blinding. We tried a scheme with fluorescent lights situated underneath the pedestal paving; lights coming through the joints of the paving would extend twelve feet and illuminate the surface above with a precise number of lumens. That didn't work, however, because we just couldn't get enough light produced. Finally, we built a separate series of "light troughs" on either side of the pavilion with billboard LEDs inside that rake the underside of the pavilion ceiling at a very flat angle. That's why it was so important to get the underside of the roof perfectly flat. Any wave, any deflection would be picked up by this strong light.

The billboard LEDs are in fact so powerful that the light on the western edge of the pavilion extends all the way across the vineyard to the oak grove on the other side of the property. It creates a perfect line of light that registers throughout the oak grove. The fact that it is such an exact line is an amazing byproduct of the precision of the whole design. When the entire project was complete, Turrell told us that it was one of the four best-realized projects he'd ever worked on.

JK: **It must be a pretty spectacular image as people arrive for one of the Stones' large parties.**

TL: Yes, the approach works really well. When Nancy Pelosi arrived at the land bridge with her

Billboard lighting with colored filters was used to illuminate the underside of the pool pavilion Sky Space, yielding numerous atmospheric affects.

security entourage in big shiny SUVs at the first party the Stones gave after the completion of the project, I wished I had a camera.

JK: **Initially, you talked about the need to keep the scheme very compact but in the end you transformed quite a large amount of the property. What caused the project to expand the way it did?**

TL: Norman's wine maker found out that there were a lot of problems with air drainage on the east side of the property, due to the proximity of the oak groves and the lack of adequate sun exposure. There was too much moist air, which encouraged Phylloxera and other problems. It turned out that a large amount of grapes would have to be ripped out, because they were infected, and that it would take at least another ten years to finally grow world class Merlot grapes. In light of that

Norman decided to free the project from the grape growing constrictions.

He called me up one day and said, "We're going to take out all of the grapes that are next to the area you're working on. All the affected grapes are going to be ripped out. Let's make those vineyards into meadows, or whatever you want. We're only keeping the best vines, so stop feeling so confined by the grapes." This change in attitude enabled us to tackle a larger area of the property and to solve the problem with the garage in a better way. It was Norman's idea to lead a road to the west side of the house. Jim and I both decided to guide the road behind the redwood trees, bring it down from the west side of the forest, and build a garage that is essentially aligned east/west and terminates at the back of the house. At that point we were dealing with a much larger area of the site: we were designing meadows, we were establishing a sycamore grove and parking; we were taking on more than half the property.

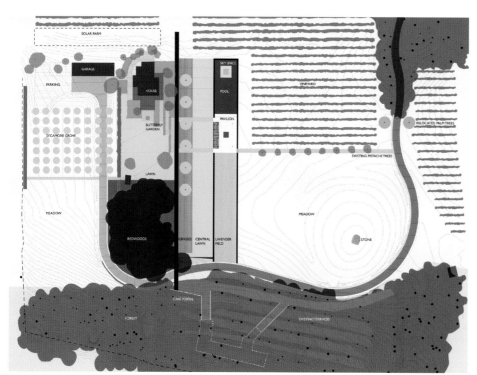

The project expanded to include additional garage parking, an extended entry drive, a sycamore grove, and the Art Cave. The additional elements were arranged in relationship to the land bridge, creating two zones of use: a domestic garden and the land bridge itself.

JK: How did the expanded scope add to the land bridge scheme?

TL: Even before the decision was made to take out the grapes, the Stones and we were concerned about how the land bridge, which was quite abstract, very modern, and large-scale, was going to look next to the existing small farmhouse, which was a "semi-Victorian" domestic structure built in the 1880s or 1890s. It had a pleasant cottagelike feel to it, and the Stones liked the house. To reconcile the two contrasting structures, we decided to organize the whole scheme into two precincts, with a central path for circulation. On the east side of that path was the zone for the land bridge, and on the west side the zone for the house, where it could exist in the kind of cottage garden it was more suited to. All around the house, we planned to create a rich, lush, and highly diverse perennial garden.

JK: Did this domestic garden exist?

TL: No, we replanted almost all of it. In fact, we had to dramatically adjust all the grades around the house. Originally, there was a slope down to the front of the house and then you had to step up four risers to the front door, which was an awkward situation. So we built up new elevations and designed a new butterfly garden all around the house. We thought that the garden would be a nice complement to the domestic zone—a dense, floral treatment with butterflies flapping around. The garden surrounds the existing deck and trellis and opens onto a very flat, large lawn that rolls up to the base of the redwoods. Altogether there are two lawns for entertaining: the large, broad party lawn in front of the house, which was separated from the parking and garage by a hedge at the far west side, and the so-called Perfect Lawn, which extends from the base of the hill next to the land bridge.

A butterfly garden and row of honey locusts mark the edge of the domestic zone and are paralleled by the central path leading to the entrance of the Art Cave built into the base of the slope.

The existing garage and parking area had been higher than the house itself, so we lowered that entire area dramatically. We pushed the new garage down by about six feet, excavating a large amount of soil on the west side and transferring the material over to the east side to build up the land bridge.

JK: How did removing the driveway from the land bridge area impact the location and program of the land bridge itself?

TL: It allowed the land bridge to move further away from the house. In earlier schemes the space between the house, the driveway, and the land bridge was feeling very tight, because there was just enough room to fit the driveway. When we first took out the driveway, we could then create a thirty-foot-wide lawn area to help separate the house and pool zones. Everybody had been nervous about the pool being too close to the

house, so we were relieved at the change. In the final scheme we created an intermediate zone between the house and pool that was about forty-five feet wide and composed of the Perfect Lawn and a panel of rough grasses right next to it.

The real challenge that resulted from removing the driveway and underground garage was that there were no more deep cuts in the ground that made the land bridge idea strong in three dimensions. It wasn't a bridge anymore, even though we kept that name. The challenge now was to make the extrusion read as strongly as before. That's when we came up with the idea for the Perfect Lawn, as we called it. The plan was to run a pair of freestanding seat walls that extend back to the base of the hill from the pool and pavilion and fill the area in between them with lavender. Right next to this lavender garden we planted an absolutely perfect velvet carpet lawn. This lawn still carries your eye along very strongly toward the end of the extrusion, toward the horizon,

Top: Coarse textured deer grass separates the central path
from the Perfect Lawn.
Bottom: Pavilion with forest beyond

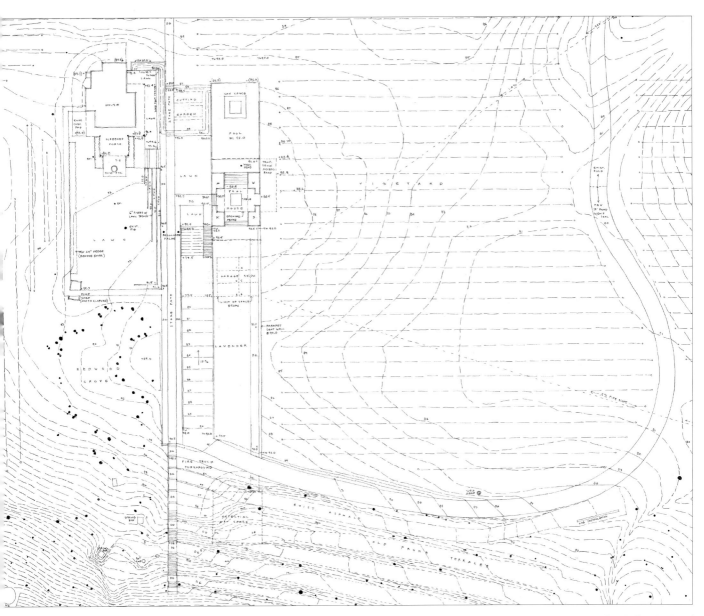

The topography of the site was altered significantly. The elevation of the land bridge provided a datum across the site while spoils from the excavation of the Art Cave created a gently rolling topography beyond the land bridge that was planted as a tall-grass meadow.

Top: A lavender garden paralleled by the Perfect Lawn extends from the pool pavilion to the base of the redwood slope.

Bottom: The lavender garden is contained by two low seat walls that align with the outside edge of the pool. The top of the walls is level with the surface of the water, creating a datum across the site and a false horizon extending to the first Sky Space.

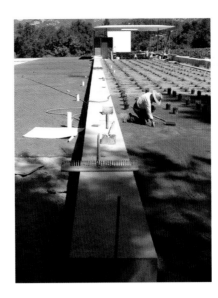

and provides a great, perfectly structured, perfectly maintained surface for entertaining.

JK: **The lavender garden next to the lawn feels like another perfect plane.**

TL: We thought of lavender because it would make a perfect linear vegetative mat, again something very flat. We emphasized to the clients how important it was that the lavender plants be sheared off exactly at the height of the walls, so it could become a big, perfect, beautiful-smelling lavender color mat. We actually had to plant the lavender twice. The first time we planted it on a grid with about twenty-four-inch-wide spacing, which turned out to be too far apart. With masses of lavender you always get a certain number of fatalities because the plants are so sensitive about drainage. There were varying drainage problems within the subsoil there, which is all volcanic ash. In addition, groundwater from the hillside saturated the soil at the base of the hill at different times of the year; about a third of the lavender died from that. Eventually, we decided to start over and plant the lavender on long, elevated berms that were about eighteen inches high. That is how lavender is grown in France, with the elevated berms helping deal with the drainage. The linear berms were a much better arrangement—they felt less decorative and more purposeful as they referenced the cultivation—of wine grapes—that was taking place on the property.

JK: **All the planar elements certainly convey the sense of flatness on the land bridge, but how did you address grade around the bar itself?**

TL: The Perfect Lawn starts out perfectly flat at 90.5 feet. The datum of the seat walls and pool also hold an elevation as they extend to the horizon. As you move from the house to the pool area,

Broad steps ease the transition from the existing farm house to the Perfect Lawn. Decomposed granite landings and the flagstone central path parallel the house and pool, reinforcing the separation between the domestic garden zone and the land bridge.

there are small sets of stairs that descend as you cross each band of planting to the elevation of the pool pavilion. Two paths cross the intermediary zone leading to the pool pavilion. Along the land bridge, at the point where the northernmost of the two paths crosses the lawn, the plane of the lawn starts to slope down at a 7-percent grade. The Perfect Lawn continues to slope down to the end of the pool, where it exposes about seven feet of concrete. As you walk on the Perfect Lawn from the base of the hill toward the pavilion, the effect is that it all looks flat. But when you move closer, all the elements that create a false horizon at the back of the pool end, and the slope of the site is revealed, creating the effect of the plane of water rising out of the ground.

That tilting plane helped make the extrusion strong. Lifting the land bridge out of the ground implied that it was a much deeper kind of structure. It is only toward the end that you see it all revealed. We worked hard to preserve this

idea through all of the different iterations of the scheme. I don't think Turrell remembered that part later on. After it was all built, he visited the site and had forgotten about the tilt. He started probing, "Is this right? Is it supposed to be so low? I thought we were keeping this up?" That was a nervous moment for me.

JK: **This misunderstanding demonstrates how even the most fundamental of details can be seen or understood differently when you work with a number of collaborators. As the scheme and program for the pool pavilion evolved, what were the elements that you guarded the most and that defined how you saw the project?**

TL: A lot of things changed during the design process, but one central thing that stayed constant was the land bridge and the central path, as well as the idea of the two domains. We never wavered from that. Many other conditions were altered

The tilt of the Perfect Lawn creates the illusion of the pool rising out of the ground.

dramatically, but the land bridge was one of those Dan Kiley moments where you just suddenly know—your body knows—that to drop that long extrusion across the ground like a redwood tree being felled is the right thing to do. For me those were the most important aspects of the whole scheme, the central path and the land bridge.

A Matter of Inches

Linda Jewell

A hallmark of Tom Leader's young practice is its commitment to both experimentation and the careful actualization of built landscapes. In the best of his work, Leader accomplishes a balance of both—beautiful craft reinforces academic investigation and tight details proceed from posing broad hypotheticals. Yet the question remains, how does he achieve both invention and mastery?

Leader himself hints at the answer earlier in this text when he discusses his admiration for Dan Kiley and Robert Irwin. He notes how Kiley compared the "conditioning" of a designer to that of an athlete, arguing that a landscape architect must practice the craft of designing until his or her responses are so ingrained that they become physical, like a skier's. Leader also discusses his fascination with Irwin's method, how the painter stares at a canvas until any ego-based interests are replaced by "the line, the light, and the surface." Irwin could then locate a line "by a matter of inches."

With Irwin's method in mind, Leader has actively participated in open design competitions and gallery exhibitions. Most landscape architects who pursue such efforts are academicians who rely on the publication of theoretical propositions rather than built projects to further their ideas. Leader has never held a long-term academic appointment. Instead, he spent sixteen years in the various offices of Peter Walker, where he learned to craft landscape experiences through fine-grain detailing, mock-ups, and construction observation. During his free evenings and weekends, he worked in his basement on design studies and competitions. In his view, the value of these non-built projects was to "have thought systematically, deeply, and compulsively… so that you can finally act intuitively."

As a result of these influences, Leader pursued a kind of Kiley-Irwin hybrid, developing his design "conditioning" at his day job while pursuing investigative, analytical "staring" at night. Since opening his own firm in 2001, he has sought to translate experimental work into built landscapes through an academic practice, similar to the way his colleagues pursue speculative projects while from positions in academica. But Tom Leader Studio pursues experimental projects not simply for the sake of experimentation, but as a testing ground for future built work.

One such work was the *Coastlines* project along the waterfront in Berkeley, California. Here, Leader and his collaborators, Anu Mathur and Dilip da Cunha, conceived an installation to communicate the composition of the underlying artificial fill along the San Francisco Bay. Although the project's intentions were admirable, the installation did not distinguish itself as unique from surrounding everyday artifacts. Passers-by often mistook it for an unfinished construction site. The success or failure of *Coastlines*, however, is far less revealing of Leader as a designer than is his thoughtful critique of its physicality. He robustly questions what modifications might

have given it greater presence, asking, "Would a shorter length, more debris in the cavity, different materials, or perhaps a taller enclosure, have more clearly conveyed our intent?" Leader seems to relish such lessons of failure as opportunities to further his quest for objective evaluation. Like Irwin, he puts aside a project's aspirations to evaluate only its articulation, inch by inch.

The core design strategy behind *Coastlines*—a regularized datum—is a recurring feature that Leader has applied to a range of projects. His repeated use of a datum to contrast the eccentric geometries of both collected materials and landscapes has provided a consistent lens through which he critiques his own work. His years of crafting built work have given him a sense of when these wide-ranging datums can work as both conceptual intention and physical object; he also understands that the success of one relies on the success of the other.

This duality of intention and articulation merged in the Napa Valley, where Leader addressed the disparate landscape features that became the Pool Pavilion Forest. From his first trip to the site, he knew he had to resolve the conflicting imagery of a rustic farmstead and the simple cube required for a James Turrell Sky Space. By introducing a 320-foot-long north-south path as a line of demarcation between the farmhouse and the sculpture, he established a zone east of the path for the minimalist cube, pool, and entertainment pavilion. The path became a datum that took on added importance as it expanded to include the land bridge, lawn, and lavender rows. A strict linear geometry meshes these elements into a single powerful datum that unifies the site and reframes the features that he deftly avoided altering: an existing redwood grove, a terraced hillside, the farmhouse, and grapevines.

To insure that this datum both preserved and underscored the site's existing character, it required the kind of exactitude that characterized Leader's experience working with Walker. He began the process by standing in the grapevines with a long-handled shovel over his head while Turrell and the client sat on the farmhouse porch looking across the site. By moving the shovel handle up and down against the view of the vines beyond, they set the vertical parameters for the pool. Then he developed a complex grading plan that located the water surface flush with the top of the walls without compromising the desired view. This plan set the elevation of the lawn to avoid disturbing the grapevines, positioned the walls at a comfortable seat height, and created a clever sequence of steps up to the farmhouse without triggering an intrusive handrail requirement.

A similar exactitude was needed to address the contrastive materialities of the old farmhouse and the new sleek spaces. For instance, the ground plane of the pavilion features a strict grid of grayish paving stone, while the farmhouse paths are gravel. Leader's material choice for the path between these two zones nods to both the vernacular farm and the minimalism of the pavilion. This new path is made from irregularly shaped, warm-colored stone pavers that reflect the rustic farmstead, but it is also perfectly straight, with sharp edges that parallel the strict lines of the pavilion. When viewed from the pool complex, the irregular shapes of the stones nearly disappear thanks to narrow mortar joints that match the stone's color.

Designing a landscape for construction and habitation adds a layer that is not always a factor for academics and competition juries: a client. Accommodating the values of a client requires attention to the ground-level experience as well as conceptual intentions. Throughout the Pavilion project, the client's programmatic changes came and went, but Leader found new ways for his essential design ideas to abide and even increase

in sophistication and clarity. His conditioning prepared him to intuit what would work or not work, and how it all would be experienced at eye level.

Although an on-the-ground experience can sometimes demand the meticulous craft of the Napa datum, it is equally important to know where a landscape's idiosyncrasies should remain untouched. As opposed to building architecture, designing in the outdoors is not always about the inches per se, but rather understanding when inches matter and when they do not. When should a designer rigidly control a dimensional outcome and when should the unpredictability of landscape systems prevail? In the still-developing portfolio of Tom Leader Studio, there is mounting evidence for the success of Leader's strategy for accommodating both crafted precision and idiosyncrasy. His rigorous application of a datum provides a mechanism for Leader to delineate where precision matters and where the site's inherent qualities should supersede carefully constructed intervention.

Leader has applied this framework to a range of projects, including the 4,500-acre Shelby Farms competition. There he emphasized the lines of levees as a datum for viewers to understand the vast site while allowing flexibility in the development of the landscape beyond. Although this proposal will remain unrealized, construction is under way on Leader's design for the 21-acre Railroad Park in Birmingham. Here, Leader engaged the preexisting rail line as a datum for viewing and understanding this urban site, as well as the history and culture of the surrounding community. These new projects show promise, but it is the completed Pool Pavilion Forest that is Leader's calling card approach. The studio's most significant built work thus far, this project reveals how Leader's design intentions can stretch from broad strokes to fine details without compromising the idiosyncratic qualities of a site.

The experience of moving through Leader's design at the Napa site is testament to the potential inherent in achieving such a balance. From the Pool Pavilion, visitors get a glimpse of the majestic redwoods that rise more that one hundred feet above the site. The tops of these trees intrude into the edge of Turrell's Sky Space where they enhance the spiritual impact of this powerful sculpture. Likewise, these primordial trees, viewed against the sleek lines of the Pavilion, are imbued with a vivid new presence that emphasizes their eccentric nature. The beauty of the grove and other landscape features co-exist with the new space thanks to Leader's crafty, laborious grading plan that avoided disturbing them. Here, it was a matter of inches that allowed the idiosyncratic to flourish. For now, Pool Pavilion Forest defines the position of Leader's practice in contemporary landscape architecture as a rare, but critical balance of wild invention and finely tuned mastery.

Credits

Shelby Farms Park Competition
Memphis, Tennessee

CLIENT
Shelby Farms Park Conservancy

LANDSCAPE ARCHITECT
Tom Leader Studio (Tom Leader, Akiko Ono, Sara Peschel, Gabe Meil, Sarah Cowles Gerhan, Roman Chiu, Laura Gomez, Nick Glase)

ARCHITECTURE
Buildingstudio (Coleman Coker)

ECOLOGY
Applied Ecological Services (Steven Apfelbaum)

ENGINEERING
Arup San Francisco

ECONOMICS
Consultecon (Tom Martin)

CIVIC POLICY
Smart City Consulting (Tom Jones)

Railroad Park
Birmingham, Alabama

CLIENT
City of Birmingham

CONSTRUCTION
2009–2010

LANDSCAPE ARCHITECT
Tom Leader Studio (Tom Leader, Akiko Ono, Sara Peschel, Gabe Meil, Sarah Cowles Gerhan, Roman Chiu, Laura Gomez, Nick Glase)

ARCHITECT
GA Architecture Studio
HKW Associates

ELECTRICAL ENGINEERING
Khafra

LOCAL LANDSCAPE ARCHITECTS
Macknalley/Ross Design

HYDROLOGY
Walter Schoel Engineering Company

Pool Pavilion Forest
Napa Valley, California

CLIENT
Norman and Norah Stone

CONSTRUCTION
2002–2007

LANDSCAPE ARCHITECT
Tom Leader Studio (Tom Leader,
Philippe Coignet, Akiko Ono,
Ryosuke Shimoda)

ARTIST
James Turrell

POOL PAVILION ARCHITECT
Jim Jennings Architecture (Jim
Jennings, Paul Burgin, Ross
Hummel)

ART CAVE ARCHITECT
Bade Stageberg Cox (Martin Cox,
Tim Bade, Jane Stageberg)

STRUCTURAL ENGINEER
Endres Ware (Paul Endres, Robo
Gerson)

CIVIL ENGINEER
Reicher Spence

LIGHTING ENGINEER
Dan Dodt

LANDSCAPE CONSULTANT
Meyer Silberberg (David Meyer)

GENERAL CONTRACTOR
Behler Construction (Mike Behler,
Sid Behler)

LANDSCAPE CONTRACTOR
JLP Landscape

AWARDS
ASLA Honor Award 2009

Bibliography

Betsky, Aaron. "Centering the Civic: GSA Breaks New Ground: Redesign of the Plaza at the Phillip Burton Federal Building in San Francisco." *Competitions* (Winter 1996–97): 4–15.

Bonetti, David. "Revealing and Healing the Earth: SFMOMA Show at Five Bay Area Sites Reveals Hidden or Buried Aspects of the Land." *San Francisco Chronicle*, May 9, 2001.

Coman, Victoria L. "Railroad Park Called a 'Civic Living Room,' Designer Known for Fusing Industry, Nature." *Birmingham News*, October 14, 2006.

Deitz, Paula. "Revelatory Landscapes [Exhibition Review]." *The Architectural Review* (October 2001): 28–29.

Diamond, Beth. "Revelatory Landscapes: Exploring New Territories [Exhibition Review]." *Landscape Journal* 21, no. 1 (2002): 214–19.

Dunlap, David W. "Postings: Design Competition for Transforming Fresh Kills Landfill; Planning Ahead, Looking Back." *New York Times*, October 28, 2001.

"Fresh Kills: Landfill to Landscape." *Praxis: Journal of Writing + Building*, no. 4 (2002): 40–47.

"Fusion Landscapes: From the Integration of Landscape Design and Environmental Installation Comes a New Art Form." *Landscape Architecture Magazine* (May 2001): 12, 14.

Haddad, Laura. "Olympic Sculpture Park (Seattle): Lead Designer Finalists' Presentations." *Arcade* 19, no. 4 (Spring 2001): 8.

Hall, Christopher. "Avant-Green: Landscaping as a Fine Art." *New York Times*, August 15, 2004.

Helfand, Glen. "Strange Terrain." *Architecture* 90, no. 9 (September 2001): 74–75.

Huang, Jian-Min. "Azalea Springs Vineyard." *Dialogue Magazine, Taiwan* (Fall 2003).

Keeney, Gavin. "A Benign Visage for Capitalism's Golgotha: Fresh Kills, Where All That Solid Waste Melts into The Landscape." *Competitions* (Summer 2002): 28–41, 58.

Kerr, Laurie. "Tying Down Gulliver: The Fresh Kills Design Competition." *Oculus* 64, no. 7–8 (Mar.–Apr. 2002): 8–9.

Khemsurov, Monica. "Messing With Perfection: Eight Proposals to Ornament The Farnsworth House." *ID: Magazine of International Design* (April 2007): 76–83.

King, John. "Design Teams Can Enter Rising Tides Contest." *San Francisco Chronicle*, May 12, 2009.

King, John. "Plan C: Architects: Skidmore, Owings & Merrill." *San Francisco Chronicle*, August 12, 2007.

King, John. "Sketches in Time: Futures of N.Y., Architecture Rest on Plans for Trade Center Site." *San Francisco Chronicle*, December 17, 2002.

Kogod, Lauren, and Michael Osman. "Girding the Grid: Abstraction and Figuration at

Ground Zero." *Grey Room* (Fall 2003): 108–21.

Krinke, Rebecca. "Fresh Ideas?" *Landscape Architecture Magazine* (June 2002): 76–85.

Leader, Tom. "Demonstration Forest, San Francisco, California." *Land Forum*, no. 6 (1999): 54–55.

Leader, Tom. "Sediment" *Landscape Journal* 21, no. 2 (2002): 75–81.

Lee, Denny. "Staten Island Up Close; At Fresh Kills Landfill, Garbage Out, Grand Plans In." *New York Times*, December 9, 2001.

Pettena, Gaia. "Agora—Dreams and Visions: Archilab 2002." *L'Arca* (September 2002): 42–53.

Reed, Peter. *Groundswell: Constructing the Contemporary Landscape*. New York: MOMA, 2005.

Richter, Judy. "Gardens Designed to Inspire Thought." *San Francisco Chronicle*, July 14, 2004.

Rosa, Joseph. *Next Generation Architecture: Folds, Blobs, and Boxes*. New York: Rizzoli, 2003.

Sardar, Zahid. "Cornerstone Vision: A Yearlong Garden Festival to Set Northern California Dreaming." *San Francisco Chronicle*, November 7, 2004.

Sardar, Zahid. "The Thin Line: Art's New Horizons in the Wine Country." *San Francisco Chronicle*, April 13, 2008.

"Shanghai Carpet, Shanghai (China), 2004–2007" *a+t* (Spring 2006): 142–47.

Smith, Roberta. "Fruits of Design, Certified Organic." *New York Times*, December 15, 2006.

Sorvig, Kim. "Railyard Remake in Santa Fe: Supplanting the Usual with The Unusual?" *Competitions* (Fall 2002): 18–31.

Spencer, Thomas. "Work Begins On Railroad Park, Phase One Expected to Be Finished by Christmas '09." *Birmingham News*, December 24, 2008.

"Truly Farms, Bothell, Washington: Peter Walker William Johnson and Partners." *Land Forum*, no. 6 (1999): 90–91.

Viladas, Pilar. "Insider Art." *New York Times*, December 2, 2007.

Vogel, Carol. "Manager and Collector." *New York Times*, June 22, 2001.

Biographies

JASON KENTNER Jason Kentner is an assistant professor in the landscape architecture section at the Ohio State University's Knowlton School of Architecture. He has degrees in landscape architecture from the Pennsylvania State University and Harvard University's Graduate School of Design. His research and design work focus on the capacity of landscape as it engages both cultural and natural systems at the scale of infrastructure. He is a founding partner of inFLUX studio, a design and research collaborative based in Columbus, Ohio. The studio has been recognized in recent design competitions including those for the Grand Concourse in the Bronx, New York, and the WindsCape ideas competition sponsored by the Boston Society of Architects.

PHILIPPE COIGNET Philippe Coignet is a landscape architect and director of the Office of Landscape Morphology (OLM), an international design practice based in Paris. With projects throughout France as well as in Naples, Rome, and Seoul, the office's work focuses on landscape dynamics within urban and postindustrial sites. In 2004, OLM, together with Serero + Fernandez Architects, won an international design competition for the Hellenikon Metropolitan Park in Athens, Greece. The office's work is frequently featured in international landscape and design journals, including *Topos*, *C3*, *Domes*, and *Paisajismo*. In 2008, the French Ministry of Culture awarded OLM the Young Landscape Architects Award. Parallel to his practice Philippe Coignet teaches at the Swiss Federal Institute of Technology (ETH) Zurich. He has also been an instructor at ACVI School in Paris and given lectures at the Ohio State University's Knowlton School of Architecture, University of Illinois, and Harvard's Graduate School of Design. He studied geography at the University of Pantheon Sorbonne, Paris, and received his master of landscape architecture from the University of Pennsylvania.

LINDA JEWELL Linda Jewell is chair of the Department of Landscape Architecture and Environmental Planning at UC Berkeley's College of Environmental Design. She has received numerous national awards for her design work and is a prolific researcher and writer in the areas of site design, landscape structures, sustainable construction materials, and analysis of design decisions as seen in the work of Beatrix Farrand, Fletcher Steele, Tommy Church and others. She has regularly contributed articles to *Landscape Architecture Magazine*, receiving the American Society of Landscape Architects (ASLA) Presidential Award in Design Communication in 1989. She received the ASLA's 2007 Bradford Williams Medal for her writing as well as the ASLA's 2009 Jot Carpenter Teaching Medal. Her published works also includes *Peter Walker: Experiments in Seriality, Flatness, and Gesture* as well as chapters in *Studies in the History of Gardens & Designed Landscapes, Re-envisioning Landscape/Architecture*, and *Pioneers of Landscape Design*. She has lectured widely on her own research and design work.